ROADMAP TO PROFITABLE GROWTH

John Mariotti
Award-winning author of *The Complexity Crisis*

Roadmap To Profitable Growth
By John L. Mariotti

©John L. Mariotti 2012.
All rights reserved.

ISBN: 1479125083
ISBN-13: 9781479125081

Published by Prosper Publishing
Web site: www.goprosper.com

Prosper Publishing books are available at special quantity discounts to use for sales promotions, employee premiums, or educational purposes. To order or for more information please call 614-846-0146 or write to Prosper Publishing, 400 West Wilson Bridge Road, Suite 200, Worthington, OH 43085

All rights reserved: No part of this book may be reproduced by any means in any form, photocopied, recorded, electronic or otherwise without the written permission from the author and/or publisher except for brief quotations in a review.

Disclaimer: This book provides general information that is intended to inform and educate the reader on a general basis. Every effort has been made to assure that the information contained herein is accurate and timely as of the date of publication. However, it is provided for the convenience of the reader only. THE AUTHOR, PUBLISHER AND ALL AFFILIATED PARTIES EXPRESSLY DISCLAIM ANY AND ALL EXPRESS OR IMPLIED WARRANTIES, INCLUDING THE IMPLIED WARRANTY OF MERCHANTABILITY AND FITNESS FOR A PARTICULAR PURPOSE.

The information presented herein may not be suitable for each reader's particular situation. It is recommended that each reader consult a professional in the reader's respective discipline for further advice on this subject. Reliance on information in this book is at the reader's sole risk. In no event are the Author, Publisher or any affiliated party liable for any direct, indirect, incidental, consequential, or other damages of any kind whatsoever including lost profits, relative to the information or advice provided herein. Reference to any specific commercial product, process or service, are informational and do not constitute an endorsement or recommendation.

Reader comments about
Roadmap to Profitable Growth

✤ "This short gem of a book should be required reading for every current or aspiring leader. It is the essential roadmap to achieving success and profitability in the context of an increasingly uncertain world."

—Tom Koulopoulos, Chairman of the Delphi Group and Author, <u>Cloud Surfing</u>

✤ "John Mariotti has taken all of the things that we as business owners or executives have rattling around in our heads about how to make our business succeed and has boiled them down to a straight forward, easy to follow path to prosperity. This book should be part of every business owner and executive's library."

—David M. Lukas, Entrepreneur, Author, Investor

✤ "Ever feel like you needed a GPS for your business? If only running a business came with a DIY manual to get from Point A to Point B. Well here it is. John Mariotti reconstructs the exact "Roadmap" for you. All you need is a highlighter because this one's a page-turner!"

—Howard Lewinter, Business Expert, Strategist & Advisor to CEOs, Presidents & Business Owners

---

✤ "John Mariotti proves that short and sweet can lead to success - but I would also add simple and straight forward. I took so much from this gem of a book. It's real and a compelling read. This book should be a must-read for all business people. John uses the acronym CAST in the book I'll tell you that I can describe this book using the same acronym but with different meaning - this book is Compelling, Actionable, Simple and Timely. Read it - absorb it - and as John teaches - focus on the right things and you will find profitable growth."

—Mary Kier, CEO Executive Search Cook Associates

✚ "The concepts embodied in this book helped the management team at one of our portfolio companies transform its business model from the relentless, and many times counterproductive, pursuit of sales to identifying opportunities for which the company offered high value added solutions. This change brought about a dramatic improvement in profitability resulting in a profitable investment for our fund."

—Mark Mansour, Senior Managing Partner, MCM Capital Partners

✚ "As brand, country and regional gate keepers, we are all seeking the means, methods and markets to achieve growth, but often profitability becomes an obstacle to the delivery of the magnitude desired. John Mariotti's *Roadmap to Profitable Growth* not only provides the highly visible highways toward achieving fiscally responsible growth, but also the more required strategic autobahns toward accelerating the speed in which the return on investment in emerging markets can be realized."

—George Sine, Jr. Vice President/General Manager
Asia Pacific & EMEA, Acushnet Company

ROADMAP TO PROFITABLE GROWTH

John Mariotti

Award-winning author of *The Complexity Crisis*

PROSPER

OTHER BOOKS BY JOHN MARIOTTI

The Power of Partnerships: The Next Step Beyond TQM, Reengineering and Lean Production

The Shape Shifters: Continuous Change for Competitive Advantage

The Complexity Crisis: Why Too Many Products, Markets and Customers are Crippling Your Company

Hope Is NOT A Strategy: Leadership Lessons from the Obama Presidency (with D. M. Lukas)

Series Books:

Smart Things to Know about Brands and Branding

Smart Things to Know about Marketing

Smart Things to Know about Partnerships

Marketing Express

Making Partnerships Work

Smart Marketing (new edition of Smart Things to Know about Marketing)

Collaborating for Success (a mini-book)

Contribution to Compilation Books:

Business—the Ultimate Resource

Encyclopedia of Health Care Management

Q-Finance—the Ultimate Resource

Risk Management in an Uncertain World: Strategies for Crisis Management

TABLE OF CONTENTS

INTRODUCTION **1**
***THE INTERSECTION* DEFINED** **7**
    The Four Paths **8**

PART I
THE *ROADMAP* TO *THE INTERSECTION* EXPLAINED **19**
    Choosing Targets **19**
    Avoiding Complexity **27**

PART II
THE *ROADMAP* TO BEST VALUE **37**
    Understanding Value **37**
    A Framework for Thought **44**
    The Power of Partnerships **47**
    The Essential Leadership **49**
    The Importance and Power of People **51**
    The Power of Information **52**

PART III
USING THE *ROADMAP* TO CONVERGE ON *THE INTERSECTION*....75
Strategic Thinking..75
Strategic Planning.. 83
Execution 91
Budgeting... 93
Goals, Objectives & Metrics 100

REVIEW, SUMMARY & CONCLUSION....................... 103

BONUS FEATURE: The Missing Metrics.................... 109

WHY YOU SHOULD READ THIS BOOK

Telling the readers right up front why they should read your book is a funny way to start a book, isn't it? I am opening this way in hopes of getting your attention. There are way too many books these days, and most of them are way too long. Who has time to read all that stuff? And how do you know if the author really had a clue? After all, there is no formal quality assurance for books other than the editor, the publisher and the readers.

You should read this book because you want to succeed. Most people do want to succeed, and I assume that you're no different in that respect. And you don't have an abundance of time, and competition is tough and getting tougher. Here's the situation: resources are limited; opportunities are limitless; success depends on finding "the Intersection"—that's where your strategy aligns with your past proven success and gives you a better chance of beating competitors. In fact, it gives you the best possible chance of success.

Businesses must have reason to exist. *"The purpose of a business is to create and keep a customer."* I first read this in Theodore Levitt's classic book, <u>The Marketing Imagination</u> and I have never forgotten it. But for a business to survive, it must also be profitable. That is an essential key to success.

I should take a paragraph to explain about "intersections" and "roadmaps." This book started out as "The Intersection" with a wide variety of subtitles. The more I kept explaining what "The Intersection" meant, the more I realized that the concept was great, but as a title, it was too non-specific to describe what the book was all about. Then one day, the realization struck me that "intersections" are simply part of a larger picture on what many people still call "roadmaps" (Although the growth of GPS navigation systems will soon obsolete that term too!)

Too many people get lost and wander about aimlessly because they have no "roadmap" for where they wanted to go, or if they did, they failed to use it. In this book, I will give you that "roadmap"—<u>but you must resolve to follow through and use it</u>.

Every journey starts with a few simple questions. Whether you actually ask them or not, the questions are: "Where are you going?" or, where do you want to go—or end up?"

The comparable questions any business must answer is, "What do you want to sell to whom—and why?" "What unrecognized needs can you find?" "What unfilled wants will you fill?"

Too often, companies don't start with "what do we want to sell to whom". They start with an idea—a product, a service, a new breakthrough technology, or something they think is unique and should be desirable, but desirable to whom? And why? The creators think it's a great idea and don't want to be slowed down with these seemingly picky questions—never knowing whether they're creating an answer to a question no one's asked.

Now that you have a taste of where the book started, read on and see where the book leads you. When you are done, I hope you will clearly see how to find and follow the four paths that lead to profitable growth. Skip through it if you like, but you'll "get it" better if you read straight through it. You should be able to read this in a long trip or a quiet weekend. Don't bother trying to read it at work. The interruptions will overwhelm your ability to think about what I am saying.

To make it easy for you, I have put key words in **bold, or Capitalized** them (against normal writing conventions) to make them stand out. Think of them as "mileposts" on your "roadmap." *I marked Fifteen (15) of the Most Important concepts like this and italicized the introductory paragraph following them.*

1—15

Watch for them and really think about them. If you do, you'll get it. You'll find the treasure, Profitable Growth where the four paths on the Roadmap come together—at the Intersection.

HAPPY HUNTING!

INTRODUCTION

> *"Talent hits a target no one else can hit;*
> *genius hits a target no one else can see."*
> —Arthur Schopenhauer, 19th century German philosopher

Unprecedented Uncertainty—What To Do?

This is a time like no other. The speed at which change occurs is greater than ever before—and it is accelerating. Available information is growing exponentially, but access to information doesn't necessarily inform us how to use it more effectively. I contend it is because of a lack of focus. It's because too much information flowing like a flood over the airwaves can be as disabling as too little information. Information resources need to use the technology available to make sorting and focusing easier. Some are starting to do this, but it is a critical need in every field.

Focus Is Critical; Prioritization Is The Challenge

In the business world, as in life, the hardest thing to do is cut through the clutter to the truly important parts, and then make those difficult decisions about what comes first, second, third, or not at all. Prioritization is the most critical, yet the most difficult decision people face in their work and their lives. The "urgent" gets in the way of the "important." Problems obscure opportunities. It's incredibly difficult to hit a target that you never bothered to choose. And yet, day in and day out that is what most people try to do.

> ✦ *Problems obscure opportunities.*

You find the answers where? —At the "Intersection."

While I primarily discuss how companies can use the Roadmap to find Profitable Growth and success at the Intersection, these concepts can be applied to yield individual success too. Each of the four paths to the Intersection is equally applicable to an individual, whether s/he is planning priorities for business—or life.

Think about it. Combine Strategic Alignment (what you want to be) with Past Proven Success (what has worked for you in the past) and then look for Big Opportunities (places where you can really succeed and grow) and High Leverage (where you can get large results from small improvements on past successes).

The principles in this book can be applied successfully at any level. If you are part of a larger organization, these approaches may be somewhat harder to apply unless the organization's leadership understands and embraces them (unless, of course, you happen to lead that organization). However, these principles work equally well on a smaller scale. Often, in applying these thought processes you will discover that you reach better conclusions, and make wiser decisions—and your bosses might notice this too, even if they don't realize why.

You should, of course, proceed cautiously when attempting to change the way superiors in your organization behave. One time-tested way to safely achieve this is to simply use the principles in the Roadmap and then demonstrate to the organization the success that results—especially if you are indifferent to the question of who gets the credit.

—1—

Business's Reason To Exist

"The purpose of a business is to create and keep a customer." I've seen this quote attributed to Peter Drucker but I first read it in Theodore Levitt's classic book, *The Marketing Imagination*. No matter who said it first, it is true. The first question any business must answer is, "What do you want to sell to whom—and why?" What unrecognized needs will you find? What unfilled wants will you fill?

The next questions follow from those: "How, where, when, and for how much, etc." Unless and until those few critical questions are clearly answered, every product, every service is like a solution searching aimlessly for a problem it solves.

It is important to think outside-in since the most important insights come from outside, where customers and competitors are. Inside is where you have more control over actions but a lot less control over reactions—those mostly happen outside your business.

You can't control the customer! As difficult as it is controlling costs, suppliers, employees, world markets, and retailers, trying to compel the consumer or customer to do something is impossible. They act in their own self-interest, so find a piece of that self-interest that connects with your interest!

✣ *What do we want to sell to whom—and why?*

The Big Challenge—Finding Profitable Growth

There is a common theme among business leaders. When asked what their biggest concern is or what their most important issue is, the answer is frequently the same phrase: "finding profitable (top line—sales) growth." Proliferation will usually generate top line growth, but often leads to complexity, which drowns the organization in work and creates hidden costs that undermine profitability.

Hence the challenge is not just growth—and the fact is that most developed markets are growing very slowly—but *profitable* growth. Established companies everywhere need help figuring out how to achieve this goal. (New or start-up companies have a slightly different, but related challenge—how to grow as fast as available human and capital resources will allow).

Southwest Airlines is a widely recognized and successful example of a company that figured out how to grow profitably. It has remained true to a basic and simple model, established when it was freshly out of the gate, in how it conducts business operations. Southwest emphasized excellent customer service from the day the company was conceived. (Its stock symbol is LUV!) It is that rarest of entities: a consistently profitable US-based airline that gives great customer service. Focus on two fundamental values—profitable, simpler operation and faster, friendlier customer service—made this so, and enabled Southwest to find the "Intersection"

— 2 —

The Great Idea—And What To Do With It

Often, companies don't start with "what do we want to sell to whom?" They start with an idea—a product, a service, a new breakthrough technology, or something they think is unique and should be desirable. But desirable to whom? And why?

The creators think it's a great idea and don't want to be slowed down with these seemingly picky questions. They tend to run full speed ahead to develop the idea—never knowing whether they're creating an answer to a question no one's asked.

Without dampening anyone's enthusiasm, I'd like to suggest a few questions to answer, before running out to "just do it".

- Who is the best possible customer for this idea, and what need does it fulfill?

- To whom will it present the greatest value, and if you provide it, will someone buy it?

- How can you recognize a "big idea" when you find it, and how can you know if it truly is a "big idea" or just a "warmed over old idea?"

- What else is there that is like it now, or how close is this new idea to existing products or services? (There are very few undiscovered ideas.)

- How long before someone knocks it off and underprices you? And can your idea's intellectual property rights be protected?

THE INTERSECTION DEFINED

> *"If you don't know where you are going, any road will get you there."*
> —Lewis Carroll

How often have you started a trip in your car when the directions and/or the destination involved a series of Intersections? *"Turn left at the Intersection of Fifth and Main, then proceed to where Route 33 crosses High Street."* This works because it helps you relate unknown places to known paths and identifiable locations. This works in business too. In addition to the other markings on your roadmap, you may see a simple crossroads sign like this one at a particular intersection, to alert you that this is an important place and you are on the right track.

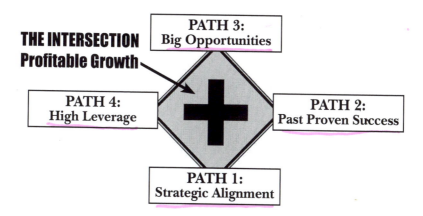

Finding The Intersection

The four phrases below describe four paths on the Roadmap that lead to just such an Intersection—one where you can find Profitable Growth. These paths involve the choices everyone must make, just like alternative routes on a map. What is your goal, or target market, your strategic direction? How should you allocate scarce resources and very importantly (often ignored), "What has worked for you in the past, and why?" Are there big market opportunities? What are they? Can you find incremental markets where a little leverage will provide a large return?

✦ *What has worked for you in the past, and why?*

More about those questions is coming up, because those are the questions you must address to find the Intersection of these four paths. That is where profitable growth lies.

THE FOUR PATHS

Path 1: Strategic Alignment

What do you want to sell to whom? How? When? Why? What need does it fulfill—either known or imagined? This is the starting place. Don't take this for granted since it defines the business's reason for existing. By the way, what business do you think you are in? What business do you want to be in? Are they similar, the same or quite different? Think hard about these questions. The wrong answers lead to the wrong strategies; the right ones lead to success. These answers define your strategic alignment—the direction in which you want to move.

Path 2: Past Proven Success

In the past, where did you win? Why did you deserve to win? What was it you had, or did, that made you the winner? If you understand why you won, and in what situations you are most likely to win, you can apply that understanding to new opportunities. If you stay close to the reasons you won in the past, you will discover your business's core value proposition.

Find the several places where you have won over and over vs. your toughest competition. Seek to understand (realistically) why you won in each case where you won. Once you know that, then find places to do more of it. Past proven success is the best indicator of future success and is usually based on understanding your core value proposition and its source of competitive advantage.

Path 3: Big Opportunity Targets

Opportunities must be large, profitable and preferably growing. It makes little sense to chase targets that won't amount to much even if you're successful. Nor does it make a lot of sense to go after declining market targets. Go for the big ones. Choose the ones that are growing and try to grow with them. If you can't capture an entire big market, go after a smaller piece where you can win, and then build on that, chipping away at incumbent competitors.

Apple did this; first in computers (Mac); then in portable music players (iPod); and again in smart phones (iPhone); and most recently with tablets (iPad). Southwest Airlines started as a small, point-to-point airline, using secondary airports, serving market niches. Southwest just kept adding more niches, some of them fast growth markets. It has now grown into a much larger airline, but it has stayed true to its focus. Aim high; go for big opportunity markets. Even if you only capture a little of a big market, there is lots of room to grow—profitably.

Path 4: High Leverage Potential

Prioritize and allocate your scarce resources—people, time and money—for maximum results. Resources are always limited. Seek out opportunities where a modest allocation of resources can lead to larger successes. That's what I mean by "leverage." Years ago, Proctor and Gamble introduced the Swiffer®, a replaceable dust pad. It was quite successful. But it was better for cleaning floors than dusting furniture, etc. Thus P. & G. slit it into a few flaps, added a little plastic handle and created the Swiffer Duster®. For a minimal investment it created a big success: the Swiffer Duster was an improvement over old feather dusters, and much easier to use than dust cloths.

Another simple bit of leverage was when retailers who sell Crocs®, the highly successful molded shoes, also sell Jibbets®. These are inexpensive, highly profitable, decorative buttons that can be popped into the holes in Crocs; they provide decoration and personalization—both high value features. Plus, Jibbets yield an outsized return for the small amount of counter space they require. They are impulse-buy items, offering multiple purchase opportunities, and leading to incremental sales and profits—because several can be used on one pair of Crocs. High leverage can turn small investments into big profits.

Your High Level To-Do List

The diagram below shows the Intersection and also represents your high level "to-do list" to start on your journey. Finding profitable growth is only successful if you win the business and grow in sales revenue. To do that, you must map out your strategies, tactics, execution and budgets around each of the Roadmap's four paths to the Intersection. Don't forget to add specific, measurable mileposts that help you define your goals and objectives, and measure your progress toward them.

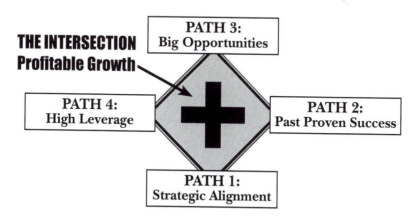

Do not confuse the setting of goals and objectives as making strategy. It isn't that at all. Goals and objectives are like the down markers and scoreboard in an American football game. They tell you how well or how poorly you are doing. You achieve goals and objectives as a result of strategies and tactics that you executed well. The metrics—the yard lines and the scoreboard in the football analogy—help you measure your progress.

Your strategy must result from a critical look at opportunities and the internal and external environments within which you operate. When you make a strategic plan, you set goals and objectives that help choose metrics for each step of executing the plan. Metrics, then help you track your progress.

The ultimate goal/objective is profitable growth from gaining and sustaining competitive advantages over your competitors—and doing it in such a way that customers prefer what you offer. Once your customer owns the decision, you own customer preference, and competitors face a big uphill battle to unseat you. Incorporate these advantages as you develop new products or services, and you are on your way to finding profitable growth—at the Intersection.

Aiming High—To Get Big Wins

Fundamentals tend to get buried amidst the clutter of day-to-day activities. Only when you take time to stop, step back, and actually think about what is most important will the fog lift and the fundamentals emerge into view. Just stay with me as I give you some simple metaphors to help illustrate these fundamentals.

Legendary bank robber Willie Sutton's answer, when asked why he robbed banks, was obvious: *"That's where they keep the money."* Now, think about this principle. How many times do you and your organization spend too much time working on things where there's too little money and even if successful, will make only minor contributions to growth and profits? "Too often," is the answer, isn't it?

If you want to hit a home run in baseball, you have to take a pretty big swing at the ball. Smaller, controlled swings lead to smaller hits. While you may be able to string a series of these together to make a larger success, it's harder to do. There are more chances to fail.

In American football, a series of short passes can move a team down the field quite nicely, as long as everything goes fine. This kind of strategy can even lead to a touchdown. But there are many chances for something to go wrong. If the opponent succeeds with just one or two longer passes, it quickly catches up or pulls ahead.

Do these sports analogies mean that businesses should always swing for the fences or throw the long pass? Of course not. With big plays come big risks too. But it does mean that a team—sports or business—must continuously keep the goal in mind and go after big opportunities if big success is to be the result. There is nothing sadder than a team doing all the right things and falling short because they didn't aim high enough. Few things are more demoralizing. Wouldn't it be better to go after big opportunity targets?

—3—

Use Your Best Resources On Big Opportunities...Not Problems

Business is fraught with problems. In fact, "problem solvers" are often highly regarded people. The trouble with this concept is that solving problems is not the same as exploiting opportunities. Exploiting opportunities can lead to big wins; solving problems merely puts a nagging problem behind you—until the next one comes along—which will be soon.

Unfortunately, the best resources (people, time and money) are often allocated to nagging—or annoying—problems, frequently caused by unprofitable or marginal customers or products. The great opportunities remain unexploited, because problems consume all the time and talent. What a shame that is.

The legendary thinker Peter F. Drucker, in one of his most brilliant articles, says it like this:

> "What is the manager's job? It is to direct the resources and the efforts of the business toward opportunities for economically significant results. This sounds trite—and it is. But every analysis of actual allocation of resources and efforts in business that I have ever seen or made showed clearly that the bulk of time, work, attention and money first goes to "problems" rather than to opportunities, and secondly, to areas where even extraordinarily successful performance will have minimal impact on results."

Using High Leverage

Leverage is a fairly simple principle. Most of us learned about leverage at a young age, playing on a teeter-totter. How else could a small child sitting near the end of the board could lift a parent sitting close to the fulcrum off the ground—except by using the principle of leverage?

Archimedes, a Greek mathematician c. 250 BC, first explained the principle of the lever by explaining how a large weight could be lifted by a relatively small force through the use of a rigid lever and a properly positioned fulcrum. This is the underlying principle of leverage: a small action creates a disproportionately larger result. Archimedes said, *"Give me a lever long enough and a fulcrum on which to place it, and I shall move the world."*

In the business world, successful managers choose targets and markets where the company's inherent advantages and prior successful experience allow for the opportunity to maximize output (gain) for a modest input (risk). They instinctively use leverage without always realizing that they are doing it. Many of the most successful business ventures use leverage (often financial leverage) very effectively. Now you can think about it consciously, and use it with purposeful intent.

Jim & Joe Swartz, in their fine book *Seeing David in the Stone* discuss how the greats throughout history have chosen high leverage opportunities to exploit. Their example of leverage using Cheryl Krueger, founder of Cheryl & Co. is a wonderful one. Using the relatively simple and scalable business of baking cookies, Cheryl's company could grow to a large size without making huge initial investments. This kind of story is repeated over and over as small businesses use the principles of leverage to grow from a small base built on knowledge and a good idea into a large and valuable enterprise.

Leverage Can Be A Double-Edged Sword

However, the risk versus reward balance is one where leverage can succeed or it can "backfire." Financial "engineers" in private equity firms use the principle of leverage to great benefit—at least they plan to do that. They invest modest amounts of their capital, borrow much more than that, and then reap the rewards. After paying back the borrowed money, the return on their invested capital is often quite handsome.

Leverage backfires when too much of it is used, and the business cannot earn enough profit to service the (debt) load undertaken. This is not a good outcome, and financially over-leveraging a deal can be worse than not using enough leverage, because it can lead to total collapse.

Leverage at its best goes beyond the financial arena into the realm of value. Value leverage means finding good ideas that can start small and grow handsomely, yielding great returns on modest investments. Amazon.com has used the value leverage of its computer systems, its web presence and its distribution network to sell far more than just books. The previous example, Procter & Gamble's Swiffer®, leveraged a floor-mop substitute into a replacement for feather dusters and dust rags, creating millions of dollars in profitable growth of the Swiffer Duster®—for a relatively modest initial investment.

PART I

THE *ROADMAP* TO *THE INTERSECTION* EXPLAINED

You got to be careful if you don't know where you're going, because you might not get there.
—Yogi Berra

CHOOSING TARGETS

Get Strategic Alignment Right

Defining your target is a critically important step. If you don't know what you're aiming at clearly enough to define it, how will you know whether you hit it or missed it? I am amazed by how many organizations, many of them Fortune 100 businesses, fail to clearly define their targets.

The only advantage of not clearly defining the target is that you can practice revisionist thinking and claim victory by definition—claiming to have been aiming at what you actually hit. But you'd better be lucky, or you won't like the outcome. Of course, in the case of financial targets, if your company is publicly owned, Wall Street will define your targets, sometimes quite differently than you might wish.

Planning and acting is better than waiting and reacting. It is far better to define your targets and then go after them, than try to respond to targets defined by others. If you can choose the playing field and define the rules of the game, you can gain a big advantage over competitors.

> *Planning and acting is better than waiting and reacting.*

Targets: Are You Like A Rhino? Or A Farmer?

Noted management professor Henry Mintzberg accuses many companies of practicing what he calls "rhinoceros management." Rhinos are huge and powerful beasts, but have notoriously bad eyesight. As professor Mintzberg explains, companies, like rhinos, choose far off targets that are not too clearly seen. Then, also like the rhino, they charge off toward the distant target, only to get distracted part way there, and stop to graze. After all, the target wasn't very clearly seen in the first place.

My friend John Brekke uses a wonderful metaphorical story in his book <u>Lessons from the Field.</u> He is teaching a CEO about the importance of keeping his eye on the goal, by having him plow the first furrow in a field and get it straight. The key instruction is *"<u>never take your eyes off that distant fence post that you are aiming at,</u>"* (or you will deviate from the straight path).

And sure enough, the CEO does take his eyes off the target, not once, but several times, and his first furrow is crooked. So he tries over and over, until he finally he keeps his eye on the distant target and steers the tractor and plow directly toward it, creating a straight furrow. Once he gets the first one straight, it's easy to follow it for succeeding ones. This is a lesson I have never forgotten.

Not Too High; Not Too Low

Finding the right amount of stretch in setting/choosing targets is an important job of management. Failing to hit a target is demoralizing. Even more demoralizing is when an organization hits a target that was set too low, and fails to succeed. Almost equally demoralizing, (and more common) is for the target to be set for them, without adequate consideration of the resources, skills, talents, etc. needed to reach it. Trying to do the impossible isn't much fun.

I used to work for a boss who always stretched our aspirations by telling us *"we're better than that."* Our reply was usually, *"no, we're not—we're just mere mortals."* His stretch target idea was a good one, but if you stretch something too far, it breaks, and that goes for an organization too.

> ✚ *Trying to do the impossible isn't much fun.*

I can't tell you how high or low to set targets. I can tell you this. They must be high enough to make a noticeable difference in the business—financially and competitively—and realistic enough that most of the organization can believe (or be convinced) that the targets are achievable. One of the most important responsibilities of a leader is to make sure that you have (or can get) the necessary resources: time, talent and money, to achieve your goals and hit your targets.

If you are targeting big opportunities, a modest success will still yield a sizable gain. Over time, you can build on that initial foothold and make the gain even larger—because the target is a big one.

The most important point about setting targets is choosing those that match what you are good at—your core competencies (**what** you do well)—defining strategies and core capabilities (things you know **how** to do well)—the execution of strategies. Lots of people can write grand strategies, but are unable to execute them. Still others are executing very well, but against a flawed strategy.

It takes both to succeed: the right strategy and good execution. More CEOs fail due to failures in execution than for any other reason. Many also fail because they don't have the necessary resources. Leaders (at all levels) *must* assure that they have the experience, skills, talents, staffing, customers, contacts, structure—and resources—to hit the target they set. To do anything else is just foolish.

Understanding Past Proven Success

Take a couple of minutes to think; I mean to really concentrate. What is my target? Is it the right one? Do I have the necessary time, talent and resources to hit that target? Few people actually take two or three minutes of totally quiet time to concentrate; to think about something important. Perhaps one of the few benefits available to business travelers stuck in airports and on planes is that the situation offers them quiet time to think—if they can only disconnect from their Droid, Blackberry or iPhone.

— 4 —

It has been proven time and again that the recent past is the best predictor of the near term future. Why? Conditions that caused the recent past are largely similar to those that will influence the near term future; not the same, but similar.

Here are more questions to ask during those quiet moments of thought:

- Why did you get that last order, really?
- Why have you held onto that customer for years?
- What is it about what you do and how you do it, what you sell, etc. that makes you *deserve* the business, versus all the competitors out there?
- What *differentiates* your products or services in the market from those of your competitors?
- What *distinguishes* your management team from those competing against you?
- How did you build your current management team, and how are you enabling its success?

Are the answers to these questions clear in your mind? Have you shared them with your organization? I doubt it—at least not without taking that two or three (or more) minutes to think about the answers. And yet, these answers describe your greatest competitive advantages—or your shortcomings.

After all of your successes and failures over the years, why do your customers stick with you and your product/service? With which kinds of customers have you had the greatest success? With which types of products, programs, promotions, etc., have you beaten competition?

Figure that out and you are on your way to some of the smartest target setting you will ever do. Find more customers who have similar wants, needs, and characteristics and who value the same things you provided them in the past—

quality, service, cost, innovation, reliability, dependability, financial stability, ethics, or whatever else. Go sell them. If you already do, then sell them more! Win based on the strengths that were the basis for your Past Proven Successes.

— 5 —

Knowing What You Know—And Don't Know

"It ain't so much the things we don't know that get us into trouble. It's the things we think we know that just ain't so." So said Josh Billings, a famous 19th Century humorist and lecturer. *There is profound wisdom hidden in this simple, folksy statement. But too often we fail to believe this in our own situation? First you must "know what you know"—an obvious, but not trivial point. Next you must "know what you don't know"— and admit it—then set out to find out what you thought you knew "that just ain't so."*

This is how you expand your knowledge based on facts… not on illusions. Refer often to the Billings quote and search for those things you thought you knew that weren't so. Those are the ones that will hurt you. Protect against that mistake. Here are a few examples.

> ✜ *"It ain't so much the things we don't know that get us into trouble. It's the things we think we know that just ain't so."*

Sales reps commonly say *"they'll never go for that"* and *"we need it to fill out the line"* and *"we'll make it up in volume."* Assertions like these are common causes of business failure because, when believed, companies will either fail to go after a customer, an order or a market position or go after the wrong one. Worse, they will defend an unprofitable product or customer. When you hear, *"We'll make it up in volume,"* be wary. You won't if you lose money on every sale.

Experience is valuable. Expertise is important too. So is talent. But somewhere in this list comes common sense and pragmatism. These work best when used together to make decisions. Beware of things that seem too good to be true; they usually are not true. But don't overlook true opportunities. Always remember this phrase too: *"Postponed perfection is the enemy of planned progress."*

"If you don't ask, you won't get…" How many times do companies fail to ask, thus disqualifying themselves before even trying, because they didn't know what they didn't know, or what they thought they knew wasn't so? Ask! Don't "assume yourself" out of contention.

My final point here is an admonition to avoid assuming someone's intentions. *"That buyer doesn't like us."* *"The top management is in bed with the competitor."* *"Nobody can break into that account; XYZ Company has a lock on it."* Guessing at someone else's motivations or reasons is a fool's game. Stop; look; listen; open your mind to the possibilities. In the famous words of Yogi Berra, *"You can see a lot just by looking."*

✚ **Don't *"assume yourself"* out of contention.**

Another useful point to remember was what a Washington D.C. lawyer once warned me, *"In this town, never attribute to malice what could be a case of simple ignorance."* Know your facts. Don't fall prey to potentially incorrect assumptions about the motivations and intentions of others. Ask them!

AVOIDING COMPLEXITY

Management Induced Complexity

We hear statements like "these are increasingly complex times" pretty often these days—often enough that the words sound like a cliché—but this bit of conventional wisdom is indisputably true. Managing the complexity of the digital revolution and relentless globalization is essential for today's managers. The more we learn, the more we realize how much we don't—and can't—know. As companies struggle to grow in highly competitive, low growth environments, dangerous uncertainty and unnecessary proliferation is almost guaranteed.

As noted biological scientist Stuart Kauffmann once told me (speaking about nature and science but referring to society): *"…the adjacent possibilities are increasing at a tremendous rate"*. He continued to explain how this rate of increase could soon exceed mankind's ability to cope with it. The bad news is that he said this over a decade ago. It is coming true now, as I write this.

Jack Welch noted CEO of GE warned, *"If the rate of change outside your organization is greater than the rate of change inside your organization, the end is in sight."* Are you and your organization at or approaching this point? Many are! The only course of action is to recognize the onset of external change and the threat of complexity, and learn how to manage both.

Jacek Marczyk of Ontonix (www.ontonix.com) makes a business of measuring complexity and the associated risks it creates. He often points out that as complexity grows, risk grows too, until the enterprise reaches an excessive level of both. This creates a "fragility," in which a small upset can tip the situation over into chaos, seriously damaging the enterprise—or causing it to fail completely.

Complexity often is created and spreads when companies attempt to grow too fast, aspiring to double-digit growth in low-growth, no-growth or declining markets. They struggle; they stretch; they create more new products; enter new markets; expand distribution; add facilities, hire staff; and create new services. All the while they're increasing complexity and expenses at a far greater rate than profitable revenue growth.

> ✦ *Complexity is created with the best of intentions.*

The more possibilities managers see, the more proliferation they are tempted to create in hopes of finding some mystical form of sustainable competitive advantage. The current global economic environment makes this a bigger challenge than ever and an even more tempting place to try seemingly "quick-fix" solutions. Fortunately, new measurement systems are emerging to help track and manage complexity, but that's a topic for a section yet to come.

— 6 —

My mission here is to help managers realize how much of their own pain is self-inflicted, and understand how to identify complexity, measure it, manage it, and save their organization from drowning in that complexity.

Left unchecked, this inadvertent, management-induced complexity will spread throughout an organization like a mutant vine, sapping its energy and consuming its resources without ever being recognized. Even when complexity is identified and eliminated, it comes back like a weed, and must be removed again and again. Why? Because it is created with the best of intentions, in a quest for profitable growth. Some of these well-intentioned creations are valid, necessary and important—but beware the ones that lead to runaway complexity.

The simplest example of how the curse of complexity plagues companies is in the comparison of several leading US airlines to Southwest Airlines. Southwest uses one manufacturer's model of aircraft (Boeing 737), serves no meals, and does not reserve specific seats for passengers. Passengers can reserve a place in line, based on when they get their boarding passes. They line up next to signs indicating their boarding pass number order. This kind of simple, effective solution is typical of Southwest. So is Southwest's strategy of using simpler routes, with standardized operations and equipment, which allows it to expand more easily and efficiently—and more cost competitively. Thus Southwest can focus more of its attention on its already superb customer service.

The "major airlines"—American, United-Continental, Delta-Northwest, et. al.—use multiple types of aircraft, (although some have learned from Southwest and standardized on fewer makers/models) and different seating plans within the same kind of aircraft, with varying meal/drink/snack services. Simply managing schedules, reservations, operating/service differences and seat assignments becomes a daunting task, mostly due to complexity. Imagine merging two large airlines' schedules, equipment, maintenance, facilities, systems and most of all, organizations. The larger, older US airlines still struggle with unmanaged complexity—and mergers have often made it worse—before it got any better.

Which airline business model is less complex to operate and thus more profitable? I think the answer is evident. Southwest keeps it simple. It also gets passengers on and off planes faster than competitors. This reduces turnaround time, which keeps planes flying more of the time. That's the only time a plane generates revenue—when it's flying full of passengers.

Complexity—An Unmeasured Problem & Opportunity

Few aspects of a business are so badly underestimated and poorly measured as complexity. Many companies' top management teams and boards of directors are unaware of the problems created by complexity. However, the workers typically know, because they suffer from its effects. A surprising number have done nothing to measure complexity, or remove it and prevent its recurrence.

None of the accounting systems in use today captures the costs of complexity well, if at all. Complexity costs get buried in overhead; they show up on a company's financial statements classified as variances, period costs and special charges. Rarely are the costs of complexity analyzed properly and attributed to their root causes. They are vaguely recognized as problems only when the bottom line falls short of expectations at the end of an accounting period.

> ✤ *Few aspects of a business are so badly underestimated and poorly measured as complexity.*

Standard cost systems measure material costs to four decimal places but they seldom capture complexity costs. Those cost systems may be fine for valuing inventory, but can be dangerously misleading for managing the business.

Industrial engineers and efficiency experts parse labor costs down to tiny fractions of an hour, wringing waste out of each and every task. But they miss the cost penalties of working on the unimportant or mundane instead of the important and profitable.

Accountants, engineers and purchasing managers hammer down the costs of services, trim budgets/expenses, cut overhead and slash indirect costs. But rarely is anyone assigned to finding the complexity-based causes of expenses due to proliferation, exceptions, variances, period costs and "non-recurring charges" (which somehow seem to recur). Only a close examination of line item detail can identify and quantify the costs of complexity. Once identified and quantified, you can begin managing and reducing them.

One White Coffee Mug

The simplest example of how complexity costs grow is this one. Imagine your product is a white 11 ounce ceramic coffee mug: one size, one style, one package, bought from one supplier, handled by one warehouse and sold to one customer. You buy it for $1; sell it for $2 and it retails for $4. Everybody makes 50% gross margins and everybody is happy.

Now imagine you decide to offer your coffee mug in 6 colors and two sizes, and in 3 package variations—two multi-packs and a color assortment. You add a second supplier, and begin to sell a couple of dozen customers using two warehouses to service them. You still buy each mug for $1, you still sell it for $2 and it still retails for $4. Your sales go up. But your profits don't. Why?

Has your business become more complex? You bet it has. Do some colors sell better or worse than others? Do some have to be expedited and shipped via air due to high demand while others languish in the warehouse until they are closed out at distressed prices? Some multi-packs need to be broken down and the assortment must be repacked individually because some colors didn't sell so well. With the best of intentions, you have become a victim of complexity.

Another aspect of complexity and the costs/waste it creates is that it can change from month to month, quarter to quarter. In one period it might be inventory obsolescence impacting the balance sheet, while in another it might be expediting and premium freight to make deliveries, or customer deductions for poor service showing up on the income statement. In this regard, complexity must be monitored, measured and analyzed continuously. One of complexity's most vexing characteristics is that it is like a chameleon, hiding in different places, at different times, and taking entirely different forms. Another is that complexity keeps coming back like weeds in a garden.

A few years ago, before the GM restructure, it had over twenty different door handle assemblies, while Toyota had only six. Imagine the complexity GM was dealing with. (The one downside of such standardization is that Toyota's use of common components increases the size of its recalls when a problem occurs, because the same component is used in so many products.)

Just think about your situation. You have more products, sell to more customers, use more components, coming from more places, and produce/distribute in more locations than ever before. This added complexity may add revenue, but is it actually adding proportionally to profitability? I doubt it.

In a public company, one that is trying to grow earnings per share to enhance the stock price, chasing volume by proliferation may seem to be working—for a while. Sales will often go up as complexity is being added, but it's only a matter of time before another problem shows up. Profits are not keeping up with the growth in sales. In some cases, the profits might even plateau or decline. Why? In a word: *complexity,* and the hidden costs added by generating more sales by the proliferation of almost everything—including expenses.

✣ *Clarity of focus is the antidote for the curse of complexity.*

An example of this happening now is at amazon.com. It has grown dramatically, but the assortment of items it sells has grown even faster. Its systems and facilities were designed to handle this high variety approach to using complexity for competitive advantage. There is a problem, however. Even when competing based on complexity, that complexity must still be measured and managed, or its growth will outstrip the capability of the systems and facilities. When that happens costs go up faster than sales and profits go down, as they have done at amazon in the recent past.

Why Does This Happen?

Managers and executives striving to achieve higher growth and profit goals often add complexity unconsciously. The explosion of products, customers, suppliers, and facilities created in the quest for growth, leads to an even greater explosion of part numbers, processes, bills of materials, routings, purchase orders, production orders, inventory transactions, shipment documents, invoices, payments, entries, transactions, lenders, covenants, countries, currencies, etc. The list is almost endless, and each adds its own increment of complexity cost. Not the least of these cost drivers are more people—"more faces, in more places, costs more money."

As financial pressures mount, finding profitable growth becomes an increasingly greater challenge. Doing so while drowning in complexity is even harder. Proliferation ripples through the organization. The majority of the talent and attention is focused on managing proliferation driven growth, which may add incremental sales but hardly ever adds comparable profit. Complexity management is more than a costly, vexing problem; it is a huge profit improvement opportunity.

✣ *More faces, in more places, costs more money.*

Proliferation is not the same as innovation, and neither are the results. Scarce resources—people, time and money—must not be spread over more and more jobs, items, relationships and landscapes. The organization is drowning in work, and yet, strangely unable to get the really important work done. Something has to give. The solution to this problem is focus. Clarity of focus is the antidote for the curse of complexity. Focus on the right things and you will find profitable growth—at the Intersection.

PART II

THE ROADMAP TO BEST VALUE

"Price is what you pay. Value is what you get."
—*Warren Buffett*

UNDERSTANDING VALUE

What Is Value?

"The best value wins." Few people dispute this statement, but what is value? Value is a simple word meaning different things to different people. Check a room full of people and see what kind of wristwatches they are wearing. Chances are that there are very few duplicates. Everyone has a

different idea of value when it comes to wristwatches, and shoes, and clothing, and entertainment...and many other things. Managers who choose what to buy for their company—or for themselves—also have widely varying ideas of value, yet each chooses what they perceive as the "best value" given their needs/wants.

—7—

Think of value as defined by five attributes:

➕ *Quality*—is not just conformance to specifications, but also durability, robustness.
➕ *Service*—is more than just how well a vendor takes care of a customer, but a complete picture, from the client's view, of what that experience was like.
➕ *Speed*—can mean fast, but it can also mean convenient and easy.
➕ *Cost*—is not just the first price paid, but also the total cost of acquisition.
➕ *Innovation*—is more than whether a product or service is unique—does it have cachet, sizzle, and style?

You can choose numbers to quantify these value attributes, and plot them on a polar graph. This will form a Shape of Value ™ plot. My earlier book <u>The Shape Shifters</u> shows in much more detail how to use this quick and easy way to compare and contrast the value of different items.

For example, here is a Shape of Value plot for two familiar products: Rolex® and Timex® wristwatches. The result is an excellent example of two very different Shapes of Value for two similar kinds of products. Each value shape points to the dominant purchase motivation—and the plot leads to an improved understanding and visual depiction of value.

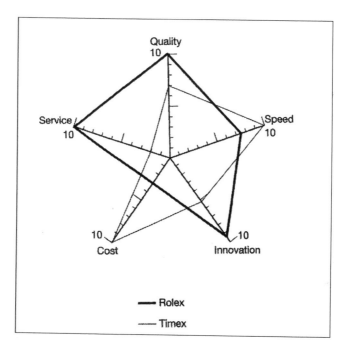

These Shapes of Value for Rolex and Timex were defined at a particular point in time. However, one of the key messages of _The Shape Shifters_ is that value is a perception in the mind of a buyer, and this value constantly shifts and changes.

If you drew Shape of Value charts for some products every day for a year, and then stacked up each of the 365 charts and riffed through them like an old-fashioned "flip book," you would see the shape shift, expand and contract—for each of the products. New competition emerges and new technologies lead to new choices, external change leads to new needs, and these are just a few of the many reasons why the shape of value is constantly shifting. So, if the best value wins, and the shape of value is constantly shifting, how do you choose the value to win the competitive battle?

✚ *The "Shape of Value™" is constantly shifting.*

Wayne Gretzky gives us insight into this question. Gretzky, the most prolific goal scorer in the history of the National Hockey League, was asked about his ability to score seemingly at will. His answer became famous in its own right. He said, *"I don't skate to where the puck is, I skate to where the puck is going to be."* This is what quarterbacks and receivers do in American football. The receiver runs a route to a particular place and the quarterback throws the ball to where the receiver is going to be—not where he has been. This is as true in business as it is in many sports analogies.

You can model the Shape of Value at a point in time, and this is important information, but it is not enough information to win the competitive battle. You need to have a good idea where customers perceptions of value are likely to be next, if you are to hit the mark.

Defining Best Value & Finding What Consumers Think

Buyers and consumers make value decisions every day. Here's an example that is trivial, perhaps, but it highlights the sorts of attributes that influence buying decisions. Visit the snack food aisle at a supermarket and you can find potato chips labeled by at least three companies: Lay's (the national market leader), Shearer's (a prominent regional brand), and the store-branded potato chip.

Which to buy, you might wonder. You're probably familiar with Lay's potato chips. Frito-Lay spends millions annually on marketing expenses to ensure that you remain familiar with its brand. You may or may not know anything about Shearer's chips, and you likely have some internal biases that guide your perception of the store brand.

For the standard 22-ounce bag of regular potato chips, you will pay (at the time of this writing) $2.89 for Lay's, $2.79 for Shearer's, and $2.39 for the store brand. How would you make a decision here? How would the average consumer make that decision? Would that decision process have shifted over the past few years? And, if you knew that one company—Shearer's—manufactures all three of these bags of potato chips, would that knowledge affect your purchase decision? (The Lay's brand is made from its own special potatoes, to Lay's specifications, but otherwise, they might be indistinguishable.) Do you see the challenge that value perception involves?

Why does anyone buy a Mont Blanc pen when one refill costs more than a box of BIC pens, which write quite adequately? Because the Mont Blanc pen doesn't just write well, it also conveys its distinctive style and cachet upon the user (as does a Rolex).

Service is an attribute we are conditioned to pay extra for. Offer superior service and you can usually collect a price premium (e.g., First Class on airlines). The same goes for Speed. (e.g., FedEx or UPS Next Day Air vs. Ground shipping).

Understanding the value basis for decisions is often the key to success. In the past, market research to understand consumer behavior was difficult to find, tedious to use and expensive. The era of the Internet has permitted the development of rich information resources based on timely consumer surveys.

To Understand Value, Get Into the Consumer's Mind

Since value is a perception that exists in the mind of the consumer, it is critically important to "get into the consumer's mind." If you can understand the Shape of Value™ as consumers perceive it, and then understand what their intentions and action plans might be, you will have powerful knowledge about how and where to find profitable growth. Accurate and up-to-date information is a critical part of any roadmap. This kind of data, when analyzed properly, is one of the most useful and least biased ways to understand Past Proven Success from the consumer's perspective. I will go deeper into the topic of data and information a bit further in this section.

For now, let's stick with the topic of value, and specifically "best value." A common perception is that cost is the dominant attribute of value—and if a prospective customer's financial resources are limited, it might well be. However, in many cases, cost is just one of several factors in the decision about what represents the "best value"—and cost is not always the most important attribute.

For example, if a human organ is being shipped cross-country, to be transplanted, speed and special handling services will be far more important than cost. When your new organ transplant is at risk of spoiling, the shipping cost quickly takes a back seat to speed and service. The same would apply if you had a car breakdown in the middle of a blizzard. You just want help! The point is, the situation at the time of decision helps dictate the relative importance of the different attributes of value in the mind of the customer.

Why is this understanding of value important? Because it reveals a lot about the "why" of Past Proven Success and helps you understand the Roadmap and the four paths to Profitable Growth much better. In fact, Past Proven Success was likely based on having been the preferred Shape of Value, in those circumstances, and at that time, and thus represented the "best value" choice.

— 8 —

Linking the Intersection with the Shape Of Value

I hope I have convinced you to think in a new way about your business. The first question that occurs to you may well be: "Where do I start?" *I suggest that you start by combining* the concepts of *Finding Profitable Growth at the Intersection* with those of the *Shape of Value*. When you do this, you can create a framework for thought that I call the Shape of the Business.

A FRAMEWORK FOR THOUGHT

Five dimensions characterize the Shape of the Business: **Purpose, Structure, Processes, Culture** and **Relationships.** Note that the *order* in which we consider these five dimensions is *very* important too, and for reasons that I will explain. (Note: *I have capitalized these five words as I describe their importance to remind readers that they are the keys to creating and delivering the best value.*)

✢ *What business are you in? What business do you want to be in? Are they the same or different?*

Deciding the **Purpose** of any enterprise or organization is a critical first decision. Why does it exist? This Purpose must be big enough and clear enough to be a lasting and constant guide for the future. This is where the Strategic Alignment path gets its direction. What business are you in? What business do you want to be in? Why? What is its Purpose? Think about this carefully before deciding the answer.

Once the Purpose is decided, what kind of **Structure** will enable that Purpose to be fulfilled in the best way? Structure is how the human and physical resources of an enterprise are configured, and relate to each other. Where will your facilities be located, and which people will be where, doing what, and interacting with each other how?

Processes come next. These are the methodologies by which things get done, results are achieved, records are kept, and so forth. Processes can often become victims of poor Structure decisions. Get the Structure wrong and the Processes get very messy, very fast. Get the Structure right and the Processes work to create better results in quality, speed, service and cost. Mapping the Processes will help streamline flow and improve consistency of execution.

Think hard about Structure and Processes and how they relate to each other. For example, if you scatter people all over a city (a country or the world) the Processes to keep them working together, coordinated, and up to date become much more complex and expensive. But market needs—figuring out that best Shape of Value—may dictate that the people and facilities cannot all be in one location. Consider the tradeoffs between Structure decisions and Process development. These two—Structure and Processes—have a tremendous influence on the paths of Strategic Alignment and Past Proven Success.

Culture is loosely defined as *"how we work together and how we deal with each other and interact as a group."* Cultural norms evolve as people come together in a chosen Structure using certain Processes, with a particular kind of leadership. The more effective the leadership, the better everything else works. Changes in leadership or the makeup of the group will cause a Culture shift. The more formal and/or fearful the Culture, the less independent decision making takes place. The more informal and trusting the Culture, the faster decision making happens because people feel empowered to do what they know how to do, that needs to be done. The Culture that develops is very important, because it is one of the critical underpinnings of the Purpose. Culture also determines the level of trust in Relationships within the organization.

Relationships are critical because no organization can be good enough at everything. Everyone needs partners to help complement their competencies and capabilities. How well leaders and followers relate to each other determines how effectively they work together and how they work with partners—internal and external. How effectively they all work together is a critical success factor, which favorably impacts value tremendously.

The same is true for how well peer groups work together. Culture and Relationships are deeply intertwined in any organization. There must be a common purpose and a shared vision of where they're going, so they are all pulling in the same direction. The level of buy-in to a shared vision determines the progress of just about everything else in the organization.

✣ *No organization can be good enough at everything.*

Certainly relationships with customers are critical, especially if you want to understand how your customers (and prospects) perceive the value of your offerings. Relationships are equally important with suppliers, because you can't make something from nothing, and anything you make (or service you deliver) can't be any better than what goes into it. Similarly, Relationships with others cannot be any better than those within your internal Culture. Thus you can see how the Shape of the Business will largely determine the Shape of Value™.

Why do you suppose GM's Cadillac, Buick and Chevrolet brands exist in separate divisions? They should each be targeting quite different customer perceptions of "best value" in the Shape of Value they offer. Each of these brands also must compete favorably with competitors' brands and models that are targeting the same Shape of Value consumers. Multiple vehicles can still use common parts (e.g., like door handles) but the end products must be differentiated enough to appeal to the Shape of Value wishes of their particular segment of target customers. In this instance a modest increase in managed complexity can contribute to a larger increase in value via differentiation, especially when targeted at the right market (value) opportunities.

— 9 —

THE POWER OF PARTNERSHIPS
The Importance Of Partnerships
Everyone seems to be searching for sources of sustainable competitive advantage. Here's a tip: There are not many of them left.

The two most powerful factors in building sustainable competitive advantage are People and Partners. All the rest can be bought (via outsourcing of technology, equipment, facilities, systems, etc.), or developed (like strategies, execution plans, tactics, etc.) or copied. But who does that crucial development? People. And what are the keys to selling, strategic execution, buying and outsourcing? Partners. Choose them wisely.

First come the people—with the necessary talents and skill sets—working together in an organization with strong leaders. People are the essential starting point. Without good ones, nothing else very good can happen.

Right after that comes your choice of partners. This choice is very important because remember, no organization can be good enough at everything to do it all alone. That's why the right partners are critical to success and can actually help create/sustain competitive advantage. When I speak of partners, I am thinking in terms of four groups, easily recalled with the acronym **CAST** (like the cast of characters in a play):

✦ **C**ustomers
✦ **A**ssociates
✦ **S**uppliers,
✦ **T**ruth-tellers.

Choose the best customers and when they succeed and grow; they will take you along with them in that growth. Choose the best associates and suppliers, and you can build competitive advantages based on their quality and competencies. Finally, we all need truth-tellers, those valued advisors that tell you what you don't want to hear—or what no one else will tell you.

If you have the best **People**, with the right **Leadership**, and a clear **Purpose**, working in the right **Structure**, with effective **Processes**, within the right kind of **Culture**, and in strong **Relationships** with the right **Partners**, good things just seem to happen. The best things happen when you have a well thought out plan, and strategies that you can execute. Coming up with those is the job of leadership.

THE ESSENTIAL LEADERSHIP
Leadership is Essential

The other essential ingredient for creating competitive advantage through the best people/partners is leadership. I can't emphasize this enough. Even the best people/partners need strong leaders; and those leaders need competent, committed followers. Elements of leadership are embedded in the culture all up, down and across successful organizations.

> ✦ *Even the best people/partners need strong leaders; and those leaders need competent, committed followers.*

If you have been part of a highly functioning organization (e.g., a winning team), you've seen and felt it. Sometimes it is more a feeling than anything else. This feeling is why top performers are attracted to and stay with top organizations. It isn't just the money, although that usually follows high performance. It isn't just the location or physical setting, although a good one helps. It is that indescribable coherence and electricity that a group of high performers feels when working together successfully in the right kind of environment—and winning together. When leadership takes on the right role, talented followers really shine. But, rather than just talk about leadership, let me define the role and responsibilities of a leader

---

The role of a leader is:

✛ *To create a clear understanding of the current reality;*

✛ *To build a healthy dissatisfaction with the current situation*

✛ *To help develop a shared vision of a more desirable future situation;*

✛ *To create the belief that there is a viable path from the former to the latter; and*

✛ *To create an environment in which people are motivated to embark on the journey to that future.*

The responsibilities of a leader are:

✛ *To help the organization remove or overcome obstacles on the journey, and*

✛ *To assure that the resources needed for the journey are available or can be obtained.*

✚ To provide encouragement, honest feedback (positive or negative) and continued support during the journey.
✚ To take part in the journey.

At a conference years ago, I asked noted leader and retired chairman of Motorola, Robert Galvin, "What is the most important aspect of leadership?" His answer was, "To take people to places they would be afraid to go alone."

I liked his answer so well that I followed-up with a second question. "Can leadership be taught?" His answer was, "Not exactly, but it can be role-modeled and then emulated." Thus the challenge is to develop leaders by exposure to the right role models. In this context nearly anyone in an organization can be a leader—by demonstrating and role modeling the right behaviors.

— 10 —

THE IMPORTANCE AND POWER OF PEOPLE

The Importance Of People

Nothing is more important in business—and in life—than people. Create sustainable competitive advantage by starting with the best people. Then find the best partners, and proceed from there.

✢ *Nothing is more important in business—and in life—than people.*

Along the way you'll need a plan to describe where you are going and how you intend to get there. Your people will also need a sense of purpose that they can believe in. Finally, the leader(s) must lead with passion. Sounds simple, right. It actually is simple—in concept. Getting it done is a little—or a lot—harder. Next come the details.

Deciding which structures and processes to use is important. Building the right culture is mandatory. Culture building and culture matching between leaders and the rest of the organization is one of the most overlooked areas of modern management. Culture mismatches lead to chaos, confusion and ultimately failure. The culture spills over into the relationships with your critical CAST of partners. (Remember, CAST is the acronym that describes those four critical partners: **C**ustomers, **A**ssociates, **S**uppliers and **T**ruth-tellers.)

Choose people wisely and well. Build a culture in which they can succeed. Choose partners wisely and carefully too. This culture and these relationships are what leads to win-win outcomes. Lead with a purpose, a plan, and with passion; success will follow. Simple? Yes. Easy? No. Critical? Absolutely!

THE POWER OF INFORMATION

The Importance of Information—Why Fly Blind?

Back in the Cold War era, when Russia was the USSR, travel there was difficult. Secrecy was paramount in a Communist country, so the roadmaps that were available were not to scale and were purposely distorted and mislabeled. Visitors were not supposed to be able to find things easily. Misinformation is a powerful tool. So is good information; it can provide the basis for a sustainable competitive advantage.

I think most readers will agree that good information (accurate, up-to-date roadmaps) combined with good insight, timely decisions and effective action usually lead to success. But what if there is a shortage of good information? People act on their perceptions and assumptions, many of which are flawed, biased, or at least unproven—and they get lost.

Most C-suite executives are smart people. Executives suffer because nearly all the information they receive from subordinates is filtered as it is passed on to them. Few subordinates tell their bosses the whole, ugly truth about situations. Why? Because they are fearful they will somehow be blamed.

Everyone up the organization also receives filtered information from his or her subordinates. This is not usually malicious. It is simply human nature. After all, aren't they supposed to fix these problems? No one likes to tell his or her boss the bad news. So the boss gets filtered information and passes it on, adding his/her own filter. Thus intelligent C-suite executives make decisions based on layers of bad information—and those decisions are either less effective than they might be, or just downright wrong.

But how does the C-suite know it's getting filtered information? Look outside! The truth, which is the key to finding profitable growth, lies outside the company. The truth is available to anyone smart enough to look for it, find it and use it. Only reliable outside information will enable executives to find the truth they need to recognize and/or challenge the filtered (flawed) information they receive.

Computer specialists used the term GIGO: Garbage In—Garbage Out to describe what happened when computers were fed lousy or erroneous information. People in organizations work the same way. So why don't people look for better (outside) information? Either they are too lazy/timid to do so; or they don't know where to look; or they claim that they don't have the budget to pay for good information —even if they knew where to get it. The latter reason is one of the greatest false economies in the business world today.

Four Formulas Describe the Relationships

After that rather lengthy introduction to the topic of how people use or misuse, alter or ignore information, I want to cite four formulas that illustrate the relationship between data, information, knowledge and success.

The formulas that follow describe this information progression very well—and they are sequential in nature.

FOUR FORMULAS FOR SUCCESS
Data + Organization = Information
Information + Human Insight = Knowledge
Knowledge + Experience = Wisdom
Wisdom + Imagination = Genius

It is from this sequence that success is derived, and this is another essential part of the Roadmap to Profitable Growth.

Gathering data these days is actually fairly easy. Data gathering, either via market research, surveys or other methods has been done for decades. The power of the Internet has altered the ease of gathering data. What it has not changed is the need to gather "good data," and analyze it, and then display it in ways that transform the data according to the four formulas.

Data may be everywhere, but good information costs time, effort and money to find, analyze and organize. The key is what to do with the data, once gathered, since data is merely the "raw material" from which information, knowledge and wisdom is created. At the very least, good information acts as insurance against making really foolish decisions. At best, the data reveals so much more about markets, competition and especially customers/consumers that using the Roadmap and finding the best paths to profitable growth becomes much, much easier.

The payback on investments of time, effort and money into useful knowledge can be huge—provided the data and its successive evolution into information and knowledge is done properly. Until then, the ultimate job is still not done. The critical work is helping people interact with the results of this data transformation. Done right, the results can be used to guide strategy development, and with critical insights, can lead to the best decisions, and confidence to take action.

Many companies have been doing surveys, gathering market research data for a long time. The big names like Nielsen and Gallup are two of the most well known. Such large and long-standing firms are deeply invested in what they do—and how they do it—and they have a large base of clients who are similarly invested in their data. But in this era of interconnectivity and rapid change, this is no longer good enough.

A well-known novel title comes to mind. The 1971 book, _"That Was Then, and This Is Now,"_ by S. E. Hinton was a coming of age story, describing how two brothers grew up quite differently, as their lives and the times changed. Such it is in this field of data being transformed to information, knowledge and wisdom. This is most definitely "Now"— and a much different set of conditions from "Then."

"Now" is the second decade of the 21st century, and we are deeply into globalization and information technology that has shrunk the globe and accelerated the transfer of knowledge and information around the world faster than ever before. And yet, some truths remain timeless. Strategy consultant and author Gary Hamel described very well how entrenched incumbents seldom (or never) develop the new breakthroughs in any field. Incumbents are too invested in their past and present successes. Hamel's conclusions led me to devise yet another formula that describes the situation very succinctly: PP*2≠FF.

This formula applies in any field of endeavor—but especially in business—and in this case, it is especially relevant. The terms abbreviated by the formula are: Preserving the Past (PP) and Perfecting the Present (PP) does <u>not</u> equal Finding the Future (FF). The two PPs—Past and Present—consume so much of the available resources (time, talent and money) that little or none remain for the FF—Finding (or Funding) the Future.

PP*2 ≠ FF
Preserving the Past (PP) and Perfecting the Present (PP) does <u>not</u> equal Finding the Future (FF)

Fortunately, there are smaller, nimbler "upstarts" that provide the new, cutting-edge approaches that the older, larger incumbents can only chase and hope to copy. The next section describes how just one of these firms is pushing the frontiers of "Four Formulas" to achieve new and better insights. This new offering from the serial innovators at Prosper Business Development is aptly named "BIGinsight." (www.biginsight.com)

I first encountered the Prosper team when it created BIGresearch over a decade ago, a name that described its core purpose at that time—gathering market research data based on large, comprehensive consumer surveys. I liked it because it offered some of the most effective, in-depth and easiest to use survey data and market information I had seen. Consumer Surveys showed the responses of thousands of people (8,000+), very effectively.

While no one can really predict the future, such a survey can show what consumers might likely do in the future. The information can be sorted and analyzed in many ways to find answers to specific questions, based on demographics, economics, brand preferences and more, thus providing very useful consumer insights. However, others also do surveys, and these come in all sizes and shapes.

When I challenged Prosper CEO Gary Drenik to explain to me what they are doing differently and better now, he did just that. Drenik started by taking me back a decade, to the era of the dot-coms (AOL, Yahoo!, MSN, et. al.), and to the beginnings of BIGresearch. He pointed out how Prosper developed and used Internet-based survey technology with special computer applications to gather and analyze large amounts of consumer data quickly and effectively.

As he put it, *"We were doing on-line research, getting great results, and then telling our clients, 'Here's your data, and what you do with it is up to you'."* The problem was, the clients' use of the data was highly variable. Some used it very well, while others used it only sporadically. Still others paid for data, but really didn't use it effectively at all—either because they didn't know how—or they just never got around to it. Thus the value they assigned to the surveys varied widely—as did the contract "renewals." This kind of problem represented a great opportunity.

When a survey was completed, subscriber companies could know how thousands of consumers responded to questions about past, present and planned (future) spending. This information could be displayed and cross-tabbed in numerous ways: age, gender, geography, income level, etc. While this was not quite "predicting the future," the data provided by consumers' actual responses were a powerful indicator indeed—IF, and only if—the client analyzed and used the data in the right way. But many didn't—and that led them to question if it was a good investment.

This led Prosper to change what it offered clients from a "research company" into an "insight provider," thus the name BIGinsight. This ushered in a whole new era. In Drenik's analogy Facebook, Twitter, Google, etc. "now" typified this recent era. As change and new networks evolved rapidly, Prosper dug deeper into what clients really wanted and needed. This resulted in the development of new programs/products like MediaPlanIQ™, which mined the research data to create media allocation models specifically for their clients' store(s) and consumers.

This was a great progress—but still not enough. Now clients not only had lots of data, but also it was translated into what that data was (or should be) telling them. The evolution from Data to Information to Knowledge (as my "Four Formulas" cited earlier) had begun to make a difference. Customized dashboards were easily developed to display recent information at-a-glance, and much, much more. Examples of Prosper's offerings can be seen at: www.biginsight.com/decisions.

A comfortable, large incumbent might have been content to "rest on its laurels" at this stage, and savor (and profit from) its achievement. But this is not the way of "innovative upstarts." Over a decade ago, Gary Hamel used the phrase, *"The power of incumbency versus the power of imagination,"* in his bestseller *Leading the Revolution*, to describe how the revolution of imagination would reshape future competition.

This phrase embraces the final one of my Four Formulas, and leads into what Gary Drenik described to me while exploring how information and insights could be a powerful part of the Roadmap to Profitable Growth.

He recited a sequence of descriptive words to share his vision of Prosper and how it thinks and operates. I want to share them with you here, because they lead to a powerful set of conclusions later: *"Small, visionary, involved, practical, responsive, useful, powerful."* He repeatedly used the phrase *"decision drivers."*

When we started discussing this new era, the relevance of the "that was *then*, this is *now*" phrase became more evident than ever. We are now entering a new era of *"mobile—on demand—customizable—interactive, decision-support."*

Like GPS satellite-based data enabled interactive roadmaps that also contained information about the conditions of roads, traffic, accidents and weather, the new InsightCenter™ from Prosper leads to timely interactive decision support that is accessible and tailored to all levels of an organization. No longer must the data be processed by analysts, who filter it and pass it upward, through multiple levels of management, each introducing its own biases, distortions, delays and inaccuracies before reaching the top of the organization.

Now, The C-suite can access its own decision support "insights," organized for its needs, but based on the same rich sources of data. The VP level can use a different, but related set of Prosper InsightCenters, with Decision Drivers—dashboards and indicators that enable timely and effective decision-making. Strategies can now be based on combinations of trends over time from multiple sources. A good term to describe them might be "outside insights."

The pilot of a plane doesn't need to read a barometer to determine barometric pressure and then convert that to an altitude. A pre-calibrated altimeter does it and shows the result—as does a different gauge showing rate of change in altitude. Why have businesses been denied these kinds of indicators? Simply because too many incumbents were satisfied with "selling data." In some cases, the client's management didn't know what to ask for, because they couldn't (or hadn't) imagined what else might even be possible.

Finally, our discussion shifted to the current and near term future era, and the reach and power of "the cloud." In Drenik's terms, when the cloud is used, everything can *be* "*immediately accessible, scalable, mobile and available.*" Displays can "*tell you a lot at-a-glance,*" but another key is "*knowing what to show, and deciding how to show it,*" and finally, "*what's relevant, what's important, what's changing—and what's not, how and how fast.... and so much more.*"

I am including here a diagram that portrays the power and potential of this kind of information resource. If "a picture is worth a thousand words, "this "picture" will explain more than any more narrative.

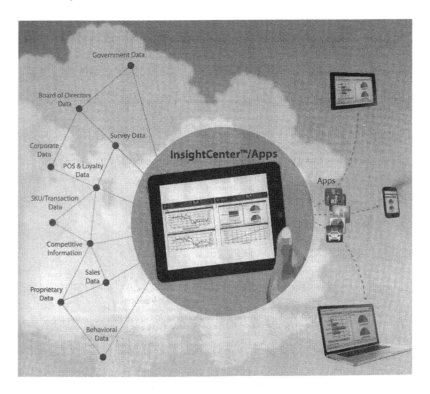

When I listened to Drenik and looked at this picture the "cloud" in it reminded me what I had read recently in an advance copy of a new book: <u>Cloud Surfing: A New Way to Think About Risk, Innovation, Scale and Success</u> (Social Century) by Tom Koulopoulos. I recalled the words from Tom's Introduction, which I have excerpted below:

"We'll start in chapter 1 by defining the cloud and separating it from the idea of a simple network of computers, a mistake often made by those who feel the cloud is nothing more than a marketing ploy that repackages mainframe computing time-sharing models popular in the 1960s and 1970s. Then we'll look at some of the basic shifts in behavior <u>that will occur as the information technology industry moves to a business model that extracts value based on behavioral patterns and influence rather than one based on devices. This is a shift that will make consumers and users experience the ultimate products around which businesses will innovate.</u>"
[My emphasis added]

Those last two sentences describe exactly what Gary Drenik had been saying to me. The pervasive and scalable nature of "the cloud" would make this an era in which it will (in Tom's words) *"...make consumers and users experience the ultimate products around which businesses will innovate. ..."*

When a pilot in an aircraft has problems with navigational instruments, and visibility is bad he is "flying blind," and in his case the "clouds" cause part of the blindness. This is a frightening and dangerous situation, and yet many companies do it all the time. They refuse to spend the modest sums of money to obtain and properly display critical information needed to operate and innovate. The kind of insights gained from timely, organized, at-a-glance information will inform their decisions, and give them a competitive advantage. In this case, "the cloud" becomes an enabler making possible things that were unimaginable a short few years ago. Imagine a very-nearly-real-time, dynamic, available-everywhere, interactive part of the Roadmap to Profitable Growth.

At the very least, knowledge about consumers/customers and markets will drive better decision-making, more quickly and in virtually every area of a company. When the information is presented in user-friendly forms, like the dashboard on your car, the instrument panel on a plane, the control room of a major railroad, or an InsightCenter such as the one pictured, management can quickly see the onset of trouble—or that all is well—and the instruments confirm this. Information organized around "insights" becomes even more powerful, as it is shared, used and adapted to drive decision-making.

When such consumer information resources are readily available, why would companies choose to "fly blind?" Or, in many cases, why would they use old, outdated, flawed or piecemeal "roadmaps"—fragmentary surveys that only cover bits and pieces of their market? Why would they be slow to switch to such powerfully innovative tools? Probably because they are stuck in incumbency concentrating on "preserving the past or perfecting the present," since those represent the core of their current business.

Thus, with nothing left to "find (and fund) the future," they choose to save money—"there is no budget left for that"—

an all too common excuse. Or perhaps, they cling to their old, comfortable, and familiar surveys—or because that old data is unique to their industry/client base (which may have value, IF the industry-specific surveys are well done).

The amazing point is that there are still too many large global companies and many of their suppliers, who have become inbred and myopic and simply choose not to subscribe to—and use—this kind of powerful information. In contrast to those incumbents who ignore such a treasure of information, are those forward-looking, innovative companies (revolutionaries) that use such data to plan their strategies, decisions, and actions. Can you guess who has the competitive advantage?

Since I am familiar with how boards of directors work, having served on several, let me briefly digress to mention the Board of Directors. Board members are heavily dependent on management-controlled, and filtered information. Of all the possible users of powerful information resources, these Board members especially should insist that outside insights (such as BIGinsight's) be a part of their reference material—yet most do not. Shame on them! Now is the time to change that.

Does this all mean that Hamel's decade-old choice of *"incumbency vs. imagination"* is behind such behaviors? Not necessarily. Boards are usually made up of accomplished, experienced and intelligent people. Thus, I can only hope they are not ignorant of the information/insights that are available and how powerfully useful they can be? Boards bear the responsibility for oversight of a company's management, and stewardship of the owners/shareholders' investments. This type of information breakthrough—the ability to have ready access to "outside insights"—represents a huge opportunity for members of Boards to significantly improve their governance and thus their companies' performance.

Consider this question: who has the greatest competitive advantage in finding the four paths to profitable growth? The company that is "flying blind," believing what it wants to believe? Is it the one with fragmented data from old/piecemeal research? Or is it the one that has a new, dynamic Roadmap full of timely, comprehensive insights on markets, customers, and consumers? You know that answer!

Yes, the Roadmap can help you find—and travel—the four paths to profitable growth before your competitors do. Speed is important. So is prudent risk-taking. To make these decisions faster and better, you need accurate, insightful, and timely information—with constantly up-to-date conditions. Just follow the four formulas—here they are again:

FOUR FORMULAS FOR SUCCESS
Data + Organization = Information
Information + Human Insight = Knowledge
Knowledge + Experience = Wisdom
Wisdom + Imagination = Genius

Competitive Intelligence

I started this section by talking about the Shape of the Business™. I identified five dimensions that describe the Shape of the Business. I briefly covered these, and then focused on people and partners as critical keys to success. But people and partners need good information to be truly effective. There are two ways to get that information (in addition to your internal information). One is from outside sources that provide it, and I just finished describing one. The other source is from "competitive intelligence." This kind of intelligence is information that is particularly relevant to your business, and informs you about your competitors and the competitive situation—via outside insights.

Competitive intelligence is often poorly collected (if it is collected at all), and may not be well communicated, either. Too many companies lack systematic ways to collect and share these vital insights. This leads them to make decisions based on assumptions, rumors and innuendo instead of carefully collected, detailed information. When evaluating how value shifts over time (as in the Shape of Value determination), competitive intelligence is essential. Many times, the shifts are caused by the introduction of a new product or service, or the emergence of a new competitor, who changes the shape of value that is being offered.

A good example of value shifts would be how the Blackberry® and then Apple's iPhone® changed the use and value of cell phones. Prior to those products, most cell phones were primarily used as mobile telephones, with internal phone directories, a crude calendar and/or notes section and a basic, low-resolution camera.

Blackberry made "smart phones" into contact, calendar, email and text messaging, networked business tools. The iPhone expanded their utility as small, portable, multi-function, interactive computers, cameras and much more (games, photo albums, etc.) Without good competitive intelligence about the pace and nature of this change, traditional cell phone leaders like Motorola and Nokia were temporarily stranded on rapidly shrinking islands of market space, while newcomers like Samsung gained market share. Their future was dramatically affected, as the new smart phone entrants found all four paths to profitable growth—very rapidly.

There are many sources of competitive intelligence. Why more companies do not collect and use it better, is puzzling. Public companies report a lot of information. The U. S. Government reports a great deal about commerce, labor, (imported) products, goods and services. Industry specific market research firms and associations offer many views of what is happening. A vast amount of competitive intelligence is out there just waiting to be gathered, shared, and converted to useful information, knowledge and insights.

The richest of all competitive intelligence sources is the interaction between employees, customers, suppliers, and even (carefully), competitors. Most of this is gathered haphazardly, shared poorly and/or not captured at all—at least not for any specific use. A former marketing executive and now strategy consultant, Jim Hawley once commented: *"If* we all knew, what we all know, we'd all be much smarter about our competitive situation."

However, collecting this competitive intelligence is not very useful unless there is a good way to capture, catalog and share it. There are many possible tools to do this, but most often they are primarily "customer focused" (e.g., widely used CRM systems), rather than attempting to collect useful "total company intel." The technology to share this competitive intelligence (with suitable security measures) exists. It is just not very well or widely applied and used.

✦ *"If we all knew, what we all know, we'd all be much smarter about our competitive situation."*

A New Tool—HOPS™

A new tool is emerging, which can tie all of these information sources together. This tool has been in development/refinement for almost a decade since its effectiveness was proven in Europe. The tool is called HOPS, (which stands for Hands On Proactive Strategy/Software (<u>http://www.hopstechnology.com</u>), in practice, HOPS uses all of the actual communications and interactions between a company, its associates and partners—phone, email, data, etc.—to create a mosaic of what was communicated, when, between whom and about what. HOPS provides easy-to-use templates in which to enter the results of interactions and provide "ticklers/reminders" about actions planned, promises made and steps to be taken—and by whom.

Some have called HOPS "CRM on steroids," and it is that, and more. Its key difference is that it is two systems under one name:

1. *HOPS is an operational process—a specific behavioral model of doing business, and a means of making sure that nothing "falls in the cracks." This especially means documenting what everyone knows, so this information can be easily accessible and instantly shared within any organization.*

2. *HOPS may also include customizable software used in conjunction with current IT systems, (but need not be used IF current information systems adequately support the operational process.)*

White-collar productivity improvement is one of HOPS more lucrative benefits—and it is driven by the behavioral part of HOPS. The greatest benefit is arguably superior customer service, but combined with a higher level of productivity. The first time I saw HOPS demonstrated (during its early development,) I said it was like "Lean Production for Offices." As HOPS is rolled out into more companies, its potential will become more evident.

In spite of the great potential information/knowledge advantages that are available, too many companies spend very little time or money trying to make sure their Roadmaps and decisions are based on the best possible information/knowledge/insights. This reminds me of drivers who are too proud or arrogant to admit they are lost and consult a map or ask for directions.

Companies that have used information resources most effectively in the past, develop in-house "experts" who analyze the info and what it tells them, and train others to do the same. Years ago, Walmart's pioneered its (now) well-known Retail Link, which was just such a system—but before its time in many respects. It developed ahead of most competitive retail tracking systems and was disseminated to suppliers, thus providing visibility of what was selling, where and how fast. Retail Link has paid huge dividends for Walmart and its vendors. Specialists in the use of Retail Link data became essential parts of vendor sales teams.

—11—

When choosing the paths to the Intersection, if you don't use all of the available options to make sure those choices are right—and that includes getting the best possible, timely, accurate and objective information—your competitors might. Everything depends on how wisely you spend your scarce resources: time, talent and money.

To reach the Intersection, you must allocate resources as intelligently as possible on the four paths, choosing the right Strategic Alignment based on your Past Proven Success, and pursuing the best of the Big Opportunities and those offering the potential for High Leverage.

In today's intensely competitive environment whoever knows the most and takes action the fastest—wins, and has a huge competitive advantage in shaping what customers perceive as the best value—now and next. These companies will use the Roadmap to Profitable Growth—at the Intersection—first, fastest and most often.

> ✚ *Whoever knows the most and takes action the fastest wins!*

Stay Abreast of Change, but Beware of "Shortcuts"

While maps from the past are fairly familiar, new forms of "maps" continue to evolve as this is being written. The new maps of the future are being developed and evolving before our very eyes, in the form of social networks and advanced mapping technology. Social networks have exploded, expanding very rapidly with increased usage, but where they are headed and their ultimate success remains a question mark. New technologies can graphically represent and identify which areas are growing, how much and where. How to use these powerful, and evolving mapping technologies is still a developing field.

Social networks may only be a few years old, yet users count in the hundreds of millions. They are ushering in an age of always on, instantaneous electronic connectivity and information sharing: Facebook, YouTube, Twitter, LinkedIn, Google+, Pinterest, and dozens of others permeate the consciousness of consumers around the world. Large, rapidly developing countries like China also have a parallel list of such social networks that are uniquely Chinese and growing equally rapidly. These all represent communication networks that are too big and too fast to be ignored—but are also filled with potential opportunities, and corresponding pitfalls.

The older, more rigorous methods of consumer market research might fall victim to rapid, do-it-yourself (DIY) surveys (e.g., www.surveymonkey.com to name just one). The problem with these "shortcuts" is that they might provide a lot of "raw data," but offer little or no organization to make it into knowledge or insights. Simple, DIY surveys seem fast and cheap if you have a reliable address list from which to solicit respondents, and if you know what to do with the data when you get it. (Most users don't!) If that is true, then what, really, have you bought?

"Amateur" surveys can also be dangerously misleading because poorly designed questions can bias responses, and large, rapidly changing databases can contain unwanted/undesirable (and even fake) respondents, any or all of these can easily invalidate the survey's results. A corollary of the famous Murphy's Law is, *"A shortcut is the longest distance between two points,"* because of the unknown perils that might be encountered. Always keep that risk in mind.

This topic is far too large to discuss further here. This information evolution will undoubtedly contain some assortment of old and new technology, time-tested principles, combined with incredibly fast, but risky new ones. Like the shift from paper maps to GPS-based navigation systems, we are in a new era ripe for gathering, analyzing and presenting data and information. The rules and possibilities are constantly evolving. The risks/rewards associated with using totally new approaches—or obsolete old ones—are magnified. Proceed with caution. Be alert, as you should when approaching any unfamiliar intersection.

PART III

USING THE *ROADMAP* TO CONVERGE ON *THE INTERSECTION*

Failing to plan is like planning to fail.
—*Anonymous*

STRATEGIC THINKING

Strategic Thinking ≠ Strategic Planning

Strategic thinking is different from strategic planning. This is often not well understood. Strategic thinking is about considering possible ways to compete and win. It is about which markets to target and how and why that might be successful. Strategic thinking considers honest assessments of Strengths, Weakness, Opportunities and Threats (the SWOT analysis). Strategic thinking considers the kind and amount of resources needed vs. the competition, and the returns on those resources—and over what time horizon.

✦ *Strategic thinking is different from strategic planning.*

Strategic planning is different. It is about documenting the outcome of that thinking with plans, actions, time frames, resource requirements, goals and objectives, and expected outcomes and accountabilities. Start thinking about the answers to, *"What business are we in?* And, *"What business do we want to be in?"* Then move on to, *"Who has that business now, and how can we get some of it?"* Ask yourself and your people, *"How can we expand the market somehow and take a disproportionate share of that expansion?"* Then define who is responsible and will be accountable for the various strategies and their execution.

— 12 —

After reading thus far I hope you are now thinking seriously about what will lead to success in your business—and what "success means." Argue about it. Discuss it. Search out other viewpoints, both up/ down and across the organization, including those of your owners/ investors and board of directors. Find the strong points and seek ways to capitalize on them. Find the weak spots and decide how to fix them.

Carefully consider the question of growth and how and where to achieve it—and sustain it—and how to finance it.

More companies fail in execution, or because they have not adequately considered the resources needed—especially working capital/financing—than for any other reasons. These are all important topics for strategic thinking and strategic planning.

Competition:
"For every action, there is an equal and opposite reaction."

For a thought starter based on an example of strategic thinking, consider what an industry leader has done in recent years. Retailer Walmart introduced a $4 prescription plan, making low cost/generic drugs more affordable to millions. Walmart enjoyed a brief competitive advantage, and gained retail market share by driving pharmacy traffic. Then competitors emulated the program, so price alone was not a sustainable competitive advantage.

Consider how the strategic market position battle unfolded during this period? How else did the retail pharmacies like Walgreen's and CVS respond? How about the strategic reaction of other types of pharmacy retailers like grocer, Kroger? Did speed/convenience, customer loyalty, and/or personal service become key competitive advantages?

> ✦ *Whoever knows the most has an advantage, but only if they use that knowledge.*

In the past, you were left to wonder and speculate. Now there are ways to know. Do your homework; use market research/surveys and gather competitive intelligence. Stop, think, and understand what is happening around you. Remember, whoever knows the most has an advantage—but only if they use that knowledge—rapidly. Once strategic thinking is completed, it is time to move on to strategic planning and the execution of those plans.

Who Sells; Who Buys?

Before I discuss strategic planning further, as you finish your strategic thinking, there is an unanswered question to be considered. Whenever I ask a company to quantify who is its competition, they always think they know—until I ask them to complete a simple matrix called *"Who sells what, to whom?"* to show me that they know. It's really hard to define and map the four paths without knowing this information. (Try this in your organization; you'll be amazed at the outcome!)

Create the matrix either on paper, a whiteboard, or better yet, in a computer spreadsheet like Excel®. Get the right people involved—Sales, Marketing, General Management, and Customer Service. Choose one of your most important product (or service) categories. Construct the matrix: down the left side, list your company and its top 5-10 competitors; across the top, list the top 10+/- customers—including both yours, and those of your competitors.

Use two rows, and two columns for each competitor and customer name—to compute percentage-mix numbers later. At the bottom of the competitor column, and at the far right of the customer row, put an "Other" field; then add a Total space for all columns and rows, and a Grand Total (at the bottom right.)

The Matrix—Who Sells? Who Buys?

Customers	A	B	C	D	Other	Competitors Total
Competitors						
You	$$ %	$$ %	$$ %	$$ %	$$ —	$$
	% GM	% GM	% GM	% GM	% —	100%
1	$$ %					
	% GM					
2	$$ %					
	% GM					
3	$$ %					
	% GM					
4	$$ %					
	% GM					
Other	$$ %					
	% —					
Customers Total	$$ 100%					Grand Total

Fill in sales of each competitor—to each customer—in dollars, Euros, yen, or whatever. Do your own first—you should know them! Fill in your Gross Margin dollars too—you can estimate others later. Then fill in the competitors' data with the best information you have—or estimates—or guesses. [Note: A spreadsheet program will compute the percentages after you do the hard part—filling in the sales revenue and profit information. Those percentages reveal the "mix-share" and relative importance of each piece of business to customers and competitors.]

Use industry statistics, government data, etc. to fill in the Total market size at the bottom right corner. Use published data or estimates to fill in sales for customers and purchases from competitors. Set up the matrix to compute the "Other" numbers by adding row or column data and subtracting from the Totals. These will surprise you too—some positive and some negative—which shows over and under-estimates of "Who sells what, where".

An easy exercise—right? NOT! I'll bet this sets the room abuzz for an hour or more. Agreements are hard to reach for many of the cells of the matrix, the GM$ for competitors are even harder to estimate—but the relative profitability of your competition is a critical issue to your planning.

If you want to go after business in a market, you have to know who has the business now, how much they have, and what kind of revenue and profit they get from it. If you want big increases, you must target customer-competitor combinations with large numbers ("Big Market Opportunities"). While you are doing this, remember that the same kind of exercise is going on at your competitors across town or around the world. Those companies will be targeting your big numbers too. You'd better figure out "who sells and who buys" before they do! And understand why! Then start taking action.

Failing to Plan = Planning to Fail

When your strategic thinking has been done, make and document your plan based on the conclusions reached. To do that, one of the best ways is to use the simple Strategic Plan Summary that follows. The terms are self-explanatory or explained in the notes. Too many strategic plans are voluminous documents filled with background material, narrative explanations and copious financial analyses. These plan documents are filed in a computer or printed and stored in binders on a bookshelf—and then forgotten. How sad.

A plan must be a living document and a Roadmap to the Intersection where profitable growth can be found. The most important aspect of a strategic plan is that it's simple enough to explain to all levels of the company. How can those who must execute the plan do so if they haven't seen the plan, haven't read it or had any input into it? They cannot; and even worse, they will not. Why? Because they will have little or no ownership of the plan. Without ownership, they will not take decisive action. The same is true if the plan is so lengthy or complex that they can't understand it. Without a roadmap, they will be hesitant to embark on the journey.

A Riddle—Three Frogs on a Log
Three frogs are sitting on a log.
One decides to jump off.
How many frogs are on the log?
Answer: Three!
(There is a big difference between decision and action. Nothing happens until action is taken.)

A Metaphor—Football—American Style (Or Most Other Competitive Sports)

An American football metaphor might help describe how these strategic plan elements work. American football teams use offensive and defensive "systems" designed by the coaching staff, considering the talents of the team members. These systems lead to game plans for offense, defense and special teams—all of which tie back to and support the systems.

There are offensive systems that use passing, running and/or balanced attacks, all of which have plays to be executed. If used properly these systems lead to scoring more points than the opponents, thus winning more games. The same principle applies for defensive systems. To win, if you can't beat the opponents by greater offensive prowess, then the defensive system must keep them from scoring.

To win it's also important to recruit players whose talents and skill-sets match the system and the game plans. Then it is essential to get the team playing together in a cohesive culture, and voila'—you <u>may</u> have a winner. Remember, though, that it is necessary to make adjustments as conditions change. If a key player is injured, or the competitor's defense is neutralizing your offense, or if the weather is bad, changes must be made. Sometimes these changes are made right at the line of scrimmage, calling or signaling a play, after observing the opponent's formation ("calling audibles").

Former Indianapolis Colts (now Denver Broncos) quarterback Peyton Manning has been among the best in the NFL for years, at "reading defenses" and "calling audibles." This ability to react and change plans to fit the situation can be a powerful competitive advantage. So it is with a strategic plan. Read the competition's alignment. Then adjust and modify your plan and execute in ways that take advantage of your strengths and/or opponents weaknesses. Even with a good roadmap, you must be prepared to take alternate routes when/if conditions change.

— 13 —

STRATEGIC PLANNING

A Simple, Effective Strategic Plan Format

Over the course of the past 15 years, I have developed a simple format for a concise Strategic Plan. It is right here—FREE for just the cost of this book. I have completed it with limited information for an imaginary situation to illustrate its use. Use it, please. After this book is released, there will be a downloadable (blank) strategic plan format. See my web site www.mariotti.net for more details.

Once you have completed your first draft of the Strategic Plan Summary, communicate the draft plan broadly, get input on it from your people, and then revise and finalize it—incorporating that input—and put it into action by sharing it with the rest of your key people.

However, feel free to revise this plan (it's your plan) whenever circumstances change significantly—even when that does not necessarily coincide with your annual planning cycle. Change seldom comes at the most convenient time, but as conditions change, your plan may need to change too.

When you write your strategic plan, use terse "bullet statements," not verbose rhetoric; keep statements short, using simple, clear, and to-the-point (action-oriented) wording. This is a plan about things to DO, not an essay or a novel. Remember, it all has to fit on six pages or less, and be easily and clearly communicated to your entire team—the whole organization—top to bottom. (If they don't know what's in the plan, how can they execute it successfully?)

✚ *Change seldom comes at the most convenient time.*

FORMAT FOR A CONCISE STRATEGIC PLAN

PAGE 1-2—Contents: Mission, Vision, Market Analysis, Size, Scope, Growth Rate, Competition and Current Position

STRATEGIC PLAN for: *ABC Company (example only, not complete)*

For years: 2011-2015

Mission: *To be the best value provider and supplier of choice to the industrial supply house market, and to be a substantial supplier to the retail channels for the same "green" industrial cleaning products.*

Vision*: To become an innovative market leader in "green" (e.g., non-polluting) chemical products.*

✦ **Strategic Alignment:** *What business are you in—or what business do you want to be in?*

I. Market Analysis:

Definition: *Industrial, commercial and retail segments of cleaning and maintenance chemicals dispensed in a variety of forms (aerosol, liquid, dry powder, contact delivery systems/wipes, etc.)*

Size: *$6-9 Billion annually*

Scope: *North America*

Growth Rate: *5-6% per year*

✚ **Big Opportunities:** *Where do the largest, available big opportunities lie? Have they been properly identified and quantified?*

II. Current Position of Business and Competition:

Business Position: *ABC is a supplier to parts of all market segments, but with limited market penetration, and few differentiated competitive advantages.*

Market Situation: *The market for "green" products is growing—IF the product efficacy is equal to existing products and there is no substantial cost premium. Where either of these is compromised, "green" products struggle to sell in volume.*

Competition: *Major companies such as S. C. Johnson and Clorox currently occupy the retail and some of the industrial market segments. A fragmented market exists, of small suppliers competing locally, regionally and in a few cases nationally, but with no dominant leader or noticeably superior products.*

✚ **Past Proven Successes:** *What have they been and where have they occurred? Were they sustainable? Are there others like them, as yet undetected?*

P. 3-4—Contents: Strategies and Major Steps for Implementation

III. Strategy:
Basic Strategies:
- *Develop a family of competitively priced and functionally effective "green" chemical solutions for cleaning and maintenance use, suitable for delivery in multiple ways (spray, liquid, wipe, etc.)*
- *Establish a sales force targeted at the ten largest potential customers for these products in each of the industrial, commercial and retail market segments.*
- *Create a memorable, relevant sounding brand name and unique, eco-friendly packaging concept.*
- *Locate and qualify exclusive regional partner-suppliers to formulate, fill, package and fulfill orders on a contract basis.*
- *Develop retailer-partner relationships with medium-size retailers to enter retail distribution and to develop and place a customized line of products in each retailer.*

Note: There should only be approximately 5-8 of these key strategies. If there are more, focus will be weak. These should be "WHAT We Will DO" statements, and NOT goal statements, unless numerical objectives are required to clarify the strategy statement.

✦ **High Leverage Opportunities**: *Where can a modest investment of resources (time, talent or money) yield a disproportionately larger return? How can improvements to past successes create new successes?*

Implementation of Strategies:

- *Hire or contract with leading chemical developers to formulate the products and verify efficacy and environmental performance.*
- *Gain approval from recognized agencies that certify environmentally "green" performance.*
- *Hire 2-3 experienced sales people with prior experience and relationships in each channel targeted.*
- *Qualify 2-3 production partners, and—if needed—a 3PL distribution partner that is national in scope.*
- *Design a brand name, logo and packaging for the product, which conveys its performance and environmentally friendly nature.*

Note: There should only be approximately 1-2 of these implementation points for each of the key strategies, to clarify generally or specifically "HOW" the actions supporting or achieving the strategy will be implemented and NOT goal statements, unless numerical objectives are required to clarify the implementation statement.

Pages 5-6—Content: <u>The Risks and Rewards, (high level) Financials, Underlying Assumptions and Critical Unresolved Issues</u>

✚ **Information & Issues:** *What is not as it might seem to be; what can go wrong? What changes can upset plans or hinder execution? What don't we know? Can we find out? What is there that we think we know that is not so? Where can we learn that?*

IV. Risk/Reward Analysis

Major business risks:

- That suitable product formulations meeting the specifications cannot be developed and/or be cost effective.
- That large competitors block entry to desired markets.
- That consumers will not choose new branded "green" formulations over similarly priced older, more familiar brands.

Critical issues:

- That the product line can be developed and assembled in a reasonable time frame.
- That the right caliber of key people can be found, recruited and hired.
- That the capital investment falls within the expenditure and return on investment parameters of the company.

V. Financial Projections: (Confidential) (Figures for example only)

All $000,000	Year 1	Year 2	Year 3	Year 4
$ Sales	0.5	2.7	6.5	14.0
$ Operating Earnings	(0.4)	0.5	1.7	4.0
% Operating Earnings	NA	19%	26%	29%
$ EBITDA	(0.6)	0	1.0	2.5
% EBITDA	NA	0	15%	18%
Cash Flow $	(0.7)	(1.0)	0.3	2.3
Use EBIT, PBT, PAT, or Net Income if preferred				
Return on Assets, Equity, or Capital—not calculated pending financing				
Capital Investment	1.0	1.0	0.3	0.3
% of Depreciation				

VI. Unresolved Critical Issues:

- Will the market yield acceptable margins to cover costs of technical superiority?

- *Can working capital needs be accommodated based on typical payment terms with suppliers and customers?*
- *Will "green" regulations change unexpectedly, negating the product's premise?*

VII. Critical Assumptions Underlying the Plan
- *That "green" products, which are environmentally friendly, will grow in importance and demand.*
- *That suitable formulations can be developed to be both effective and "green" and at competitive costs.*

Integration with Operating Plans and Budgets
The details supporting your concise statements of strategy and implementation need to be easy to find in the operating plans and budgets of the company.

These can then be tracked and budgeted resources can be aligned with the strategic and implementation plans that require them. The results from these strategies and plans can similarly be reviewed regularly.

The assumptions, critical issues, etc. should be reviewed no less than quarterly to see what has changed and to attempt to resolve any issues that can be resolved (within the control of the company).

Performance Planning, Appraisal, and Reward Systems
The specific quantifiable goals and objectives that must be associated with these plans are then the first part of the performance planning system that includes

performance appraisals for the people and the compensation system to reward achievements.

Summary

Create a tightly integrated loop of: mission, vision & strategic alignment àstrategyàpast proven successesàimplementation plansà operating plansàand then to performance planning and appraisal à reward system, which provides a very powerful and focused sequence of steps that is critical to success.

— 14 —

EXECUTION

Execution—The Missing Link

More companies, in more industries, and more CEOs fail because of failures in execution than for any other reason. No matter how great the strategy, it you can't execute it, it's useless.

If ever a leader from the sports world came to be known for flawless execution, that leader would be Vince Lombardi, whose 1960s Green Bay Packers teams won five NFL championship games and the first two Super Bowls ever played. Lombardi's approach to the game was simple: it didn't matter to him if the opposing team knew the play his offense was going to run. As long as his offense executed flawlessly, the play would work.

If the strategies are the "whats" as in "what are we going to do," execution is the "how," as in "how will we do that." The "hows" are usually harder than the "whats." It is easier to define a lofty strategy than to make it work in the messy world of real competition. Remember the relationship between Past Proven Success and Strategic Alignment? Understanding the nature of their relationship to each other—and making sure the two are well connected—is critical to business success.

Few things are more meaningful to understand than Past Proven Success. Why did you win in the recent past? Why did you deserve to get that order, that account, make that sale, etc.? Why, really, when there were competitors of all sizes and shapes vying for it? Understand that and you are a long way toward success. Fail to understand "why," and you will likely fail to duplicate those past successes, although you may duplicate past failures (unless you took the time to think about and understand why you failed).

Strategic Alignment means underpinning goals with strategies. You must achieve these goals with exceptional execution and wise investments of time, talent and money. Identifying the right talent and necessary skill-sets is also critical to executing well. For example:

- ✚ It's hard to be a top-notch basketball team without a few tall people who can rebound and defend or block opposing shots.
- ✚ It would be hard to be a top-notch technology products company without some very knowledgeable technical people—and the resources they need to excel.

- It would be equally hard to be a superior women's wear company without at least one top designer either on staff—or part of a strong, continuing relationship.
- It would be hard for a service company to achieve excellence without excellent field people and/or information systems to enable its success.

- *Your ability to execute the plans you make will be critical to your success.*

Understanding Past Proven Success leads to better Strategic Alignment decisions. Once these first two paths on the Roadmap to Profitable Growth are well connected, then it is time to find Big Opportunities to exploit, using outside-insights, market research and the information and knowledge mentioned earlier. Find high leverage ways to profit from that, using the understanding of value described earlier. In the end, your ability to execute the plans you make will be critical to your success, so plan wisely and execute well.

— 15 —

BUDGETING

Creating The Budget

*Reaching any goal with a shortage of resources is very difficult. Three broad categories encompass all of the critical resources: **Time, Talent, and Money**. That's right, there are only three.*

Let's examine them one at a time to see their relevance in using the Roadmap to Profitable Growth—at the Intersection.

Time: It is the one truly perishable resource. Once gone, it can never be reclaimed. A simple little story/riddle illustrates this principle.

The Two-Mile Trip:
The objective is to make a two-mile trip and average 60 mph for the trip. You decide to be cautious and drive 30 mph for the first mile. How fast must you drive the second mile to average 60 mph for the trip?

Sit and think about this one. The obvious answer, 90 mph, is wrong. Tip: convert the mph to miles per minute then analyze the result. If the objective of 60 mph average is to be achieved, and 60 mph is a mile a minute, thus the trip must be completed in 2 minutes to average 60 mph. By choosing to drive 30 mph for the first mile, the two minutes are completely consumed at the end of the first mile. Thus, there is NO speed at which the 60 mph average can be achieved!

✢ *Time: It is the one truly perishable resource.*

The moral of this riddle is that time is perishable and once gone, there is no way to backtrack and recover it. Starting too slowly can result in using valuable time at the beginning of a project, and no amount of speed, or money, can make up for lost time later. Once time is gone, it's gone forever. Yes—occasionally the savvy business leader uses premium (and very fast) transportation, and the ability to communicate large amounts of data nearly instantaneously, as shortcuts to make up for lost time.

However, these quick fixes often waste scarce resources, and even then there are situations where lost time simply cannot be recovered—at any cost. One of the best approaches to create a sense of urgency is to express the cost of time (and delays) in terms of money—lost savings, lost profits, and missed opportunities. Somehow describing that arbitrary 3-week delay in terms of costing say, $100,000/week, or $300,000 in total, puts it into an entirely different perspective. Now perhaps the 3-week delay doesn't need to be three weeks after all! This is an example why you must plan carefully, and use time wisely—it's precious and perishable. Even a perfect roadmap will not help you if you run out of time!

Talent: Remember the part about people being the most important part of any business? Now I will expand that to mean the right kind of people—people who know what they need to know, who can do what needs to be done, and who have the foresight and experience to anticipate the unexpected and adapt to it. Talent comes in all shapes and sizes, in both genders, all colors, different ages and varying levels of education and experience. What matters is that it is the right talent, with a passion for what they do.

Sometimes the talent needs to be specialized (e.g., code writers for computer software); and sometimes it needs to be very versatile (e.g., project managers for broad scale new projects). At other times talent needs to be well versed in the law, in accounting, in how to invent, commercialize, market and sell products or services. Sometimes the talent needs to know how to forecast and plan and get what is needed at the right price, at the right time, delivered to the right place. At still other times the talent needs to know how to make the product or deliver the service in the time allotted. It's important to find, attract, hire and retain the right kinds of talent needed to execute your plan, so choose—and use—talent wisely.

> ✜ *What matters is having the right talent, with a passion for what they do.*

But, choosing talent wisely is not easy. I won't try to cover such an imposing topic in a few short paragraphs. I will, however, offer two concepts I have used for years and that seem to have worked (mostly—nobody's perfect). After you consider all of the normal criteria—experience, education, past jobs, performance, etc. take into account just two more.

The first is to choose the "best available athlete" (figuratively speaking—not literally), from the candidates you have. You never know what your needs will be in the future, so if you hire broadly talented people, their potential versatility is much greater than if you try to pick all "perfect-fit" specialists.

The second is to let your subconscious and your instincts help you. When you are down to just a few candidates, engage each of them in a one-to-one discussion as if it were a real-time talk about your current business situation. Encourage them to provide their thoughts either on what they might do, or how they might address that issue, solve that problem or exploit that opportunity under realistic conditions.

Meanwhile, observe them and ask yourself this question: *"How would I feel about this person if this conversation were for real instead of an interview?"* Your honest answer—to yourself—to that question will reveal a lot about how confident you are that this is a wise hiring choice.

Money: *"For a good investment, you can always find the money,"* someone once told me. *"Not any more,"* would be my answer to him today. I see company after company mismanage cash and underestimate the working capital needed to support growth. When that happens, trouble is not far behind. Not only can the shortage of cash be crippling, but also the shortage of working capital precludes many growth opportunities. When there is simply not enough money to finance the inventory, receivables, capacity expansion and so forth, growth stalls out.

Thus adequate financial resources are critical to growth and yet too few plans focus on this important point. They forecast earnings, return on equity, etc., but ignore cash flow and timing. Cash is like oxygen on a long space flight. There may be plenty of food and water (profit) to allow completion of the mission, but without oxygen (cash), the occupants will be dead upon their return. So will a company.

✥ *Adequate financial resources are critical to growth.*

Plan cash flow and working capital needs very carefully and monitor them vigilantly. Every business must have a forward cash flow forecast that looks ahead weeks or months. You may not be able to forecast demand accurately into the future, but you can predict most cash flow crunches before they hit.

A final note on budgeting: Adopt a zero-based budgeting process. Use past years' history for background, but *do not* simply increment prior year's budget by some amount to arrive at the new budget. Doing so incorporates all of the prior year's mistakes, different circumstances and expenditures into the coming year's target. That is simply dumb. A new year is *never* just like the old year. If there was a shortage of goods at some time, for whatever reason, then planning based on that might very well cause it to be repeated unnecessarily.

If spending on an account went out of control, then simply extrapolating the new budget virtually assures that the out of control results could become the new normal. How foolish is that? Start building budgets from the ground up, adding known expenses. Evaluate each account/category based on percentage of net sales (or some similar base-linc) to test it for reasonableness versus prior years. Consider past years' results as a good guide, because if nothing changes, not much should change—unless you want or need it to change.

And always remember, a budget is a measuring tool, a guideline, not a "gospel" or a hard and fast set of numbers. Don't change budgets arbitrarily because you will lose your baseline; but don't ignore that facts and circumstances change. Thus plans and budgets need to change too. Some of the best budget tools I've seen define fixed and variable expenses, and the budget amounts for fixed—are fixed—and explanations for variances are required. The variable accounts vary with the level of activity, such as sales, unit volume, production, shipments or other activity parameters. Those variable account budgets should then vary with the activity levels—and so should the expenses incurred—or explanation and/or remedial action might be necessary.

The Critical Priorities

When it comes to what you are selling—what business you are in—a few simple rules apply to setting priorities:

- Quality is mandatory—"If it's no good," what's the point?
- Service is essential—"If it's not where it's needed, when it's needed," what good is it?
- Speed is a powerful differentiator because time is perishable and the race goes to the swiftest. "Too late" equals "too bad."

- Cost is important, since the economic sacrifice that must be made to purchase something is a comparative one—one price versus another. However, the best value wins and that involves more than the lowest cost.
- Innovation is the "silver bullet" that trumps all; it is partly function, partly esteem, partly prestige and partly mystical need creation and/or want fulfillment. And remember, proliferation is not innovation—but true innovation is "magical"—think of Disney or Apple.

You are living in an "I want it now" global economy. But then, who really needs an iPod, an iPhone or an iPad? How fast do you need to read that text message? Who really needs a Mont Blanc pen? Who needs a Rolex when a Timex keeps excellent time? Thus the mixture of talent—people—must serve all of these masters to satisfy the ultimate master: the customer, who is always seeking the best value, now and "next."

Execution of a well conceived plan is a mixture of many things, all of which depend on the prioritization and allocation of these three essential resources: **Time, Talent and Money.** Each must be carefully allocated to the right priorities—to how each resource helps you move forward—on the Roadmap to Finding Profitable Growth, at the Intersection.

GOALS, OBJECTIVES & METRICS
Define Where You Are Going—and How

A line from author Lewis Carroll comes to mind here. *"If you don't know where you're going, any road will take you there."*

Before you embark on any trip or undertake any project, you need goals and metrics to tell how you are doing. That's why they put odometers in cars and mileage on roadmaps.

> ✢ **Goals must be measurable, quantifiable, documented and communicated.**

Comedienne Lilly Tomlin once said, *"When I was young I always wanted to BE somebody when I grew up. I just wish I'd been more specific."* She is right. You need a series of specific goals if you are going to BE what you hope to be, or get where you hope to get. Goals must be measurable, quantifiable, documented and communicated.

Football fields have yard lines and goal lines. You get a new set of downs when you progress ten yards or more, but you only get points when the ball crosses the goal line. The team with the most points at the end of the time allocated for the game, wins! Being ahead on the scoreboard part way through the game counts for nothing when the winner is finally decided. It is simply a measure of progress, not results. What matters is who crosses the goal line more times—scoring more points. Wait too long to begin catching up and the clock may run out. Remember the Two-Mile Trip?

A wise friend, Will Kaydos has written whole books on this topic, but his most important sentence is *"If you can't measure it, you can't manage it."* Noted management guru, Bob Waterman said, *"What gets measured gets managed and what gets managed gets done."*

Remember also that business is a game, where the score is kept in money. If you win, the scoreboard is reset and you get to play again—for another season, or year—depending on how your shareholders feel about the score you won by (usually earnings).

> ✚ *Business is a game, where the score is kept in money.*

Define success, and choose your goals carefully: how much, how fast, what, where, etc.? They should be tough enough to beat the competition, but not unrealistic. Nobody likes making the goals and still losing at the end of the game. Use metrics and mileposts that make sense and are simple, relevant and a valid measure of success—or at least of desired progress.

Remember the role and responsibility of a leader cited earlier? People need a sense of purpose and they want a shared vision of what the goals are. They also want to believe those goals are worthy of their efforts. Then the leader can lead them "to places they might be afraid to go alone"—and the Roadmap can make the trip a successful one.

REVIEW, SUMMARY & CONCLUSION

> *"Enterprises are paid to create wealth, not control costs. But that obvious fact is not reflected in traditional measurements."*
> —Peter F. Drucker

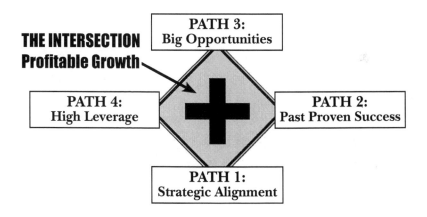

Finding The Intersection

The four phrases below describe the four paths that come together at an Intersection—where you can find profitable growth. Each of these paths involves the choices you must make, like alternative routes on the Roadmap. What is your goal; your target market; your strategic direction? How will you prioritize and allocate scarce resources and very importantly (often ignored), *"what has worked for you in the past, and <u>why</u>?"* Where are there big market opportunities? What are they? Can you find incremental markets where using high leverage on a small investment will provide a large return?

PATH 1: STRATEGIC ALIGNMENT

What do you want to sell to whom? How? When? Why? What need does it fulfill—either known or imagined? This is the starting place. Don't take this for granted, since it defines the business's reason for existing. By the way, what business do you think you are in? What business do you want to be in? Are they similar, the same or quite different? Decide and then move ahead!

PATH 2: PAST PROVEN SUCCESS

In the past, where did you win? Why did you "deserve" to win? What was it you had, or did, compared to others that made you the winner? If you understand "why" you won, and in what situations you are most likely to win, you can apply that understanding to new opportunities. If you stay close to the reasons you won in the past, you will discover your business's core value proposition. Find the several places & ways where you have won over and over vs. your toughest competition. Exploit them—again and again!

PATH 3: BIG OPPORTUNITY TARGETS

Opportunities must be big, profitable and preferably growing. It makes little sense to chase targets that won't amount to much even if you're successful at hitting them. Nor does it make a lot of sense to go after stagnant or declining market targets. Go for the big ones. Choose the targets that are growing and try to grow with them. If you do this one right, they will "take you along." I call this growth strategy, *"Hook your wagon to a star."* It works!

PATH 4: HIGH LEVERAGE POTENTIAL

Prioritize and allocate your scarce resources—people, time and money—for maximum results. Resources are always limited. Seek out opportunities where a modest allocation of resources can lead to larger successes. That's what I mean by "high leverage." High leverage can turn small investments into big profits. Turn small refinements into big wins.

 Now—stop and think. Shut out all distractions. No music, no phones, no interruptions.

Take the time to carefully re-read the above list of the four paths on the Roadmap to Profitable Growth—at the Intersection. Allow 20-30 minutes to do so. It will seem like an eternity. Here's how to spend that 20-30 minutes of uninterrupted thought:

1. Start by asking yourself, honestly: Why did you get the business the last few times you got it? Or if you failed some of those times, why did you fail? Really why? Don't kid yourself

or be in denial—it was something you did—or didn't do (or perhaps a competitor did better?). What was it?

2. Now ask yourself: What business you are really in? What do you really sell? Is it making widgets or providing services? Or is it providing peace of mind for customers, and instilling in them the confidence that you won't let them down? Or is it simply a piece of hardware, a means to an end, or a service they need but they just don't want to do it themselves.

At this point, it's wise to check your "Roadmap" and ask yourself, "Am I on the right track, and moving fast enough?" (Time is perishable!)

3. Now ask yourself: Where do your biggest opportunities lie? Are these customers and markets that you currently sell, and/or serve? What else can you imagine to sell and/or serve them? Which ones are the really BIG ones? And who has that business? And why? How can you get a piece—or all—of it?

4. Last, ask yourself: Where you could add a little of this, or a little of that, and apply some new thinking and use leverage by applying it to refine or improve something that you seem to do well already—and then sell that successfully, in more places, or in more quantity, or for more money? Pick a few likely places and try this.

Carefully consider if, when, and how to ask your "best customers" these questions? Frame the questions in their self-interest. *"What else could we do for you that would help you?"* *"What else is there like that?" "How might it benefit you if we expand into—"What? Where? How? How else?" and finally, "What is your advice?"*

You may be surprised at some of the answers they give you. Or you may find that they have not thought about these answers. And now they will. Finish with the old retail (sales) question: *"Is there anything else we can do for you?"*

Finally, go get copies of this little book for your management (including the "bosses"—if you're not one of them) and ask them all to read it.

Convene group discussions to discuss what the book says, think about what the "Roadmap" means, and allow time for questions, capturing the answers and the ideas. An hour is enough time for this type of session. If there is one thing I've learned over four decades, it is that the people in a business have a lot of good ideas and many of the answers—but nobody ever asks for them—or listens to them when they reply. (Once in a while, a high-priced consultant comes in and does that, and then takes credit for the good ideas of the people—packaged in a fancy report.)

You will be amazed at what the people in your organization know. Their collective wisdom is huge. So is their latent creativity—you just need to prod it, to wake it up—and get them to share their ideas.

(Warning: If they don't trust you to listen with an open mind and accept the ideas in a positive way, they will hold back the best—or worst—of what you need to hear.)

Remember that there are no "bad ideas," just some ideas that are less immediately useful than others.

✥ Thank people for their input and participation—and mean it.
✥ Promise them that you will communicate as their ideas are either "tabled for future consideration," investigated and/or used.
✥ And by all means—keep that promise and tell them what happened as a result of their input.
✥ Then line up their best ideas, make plans, set goals, and start taking action.

(Also remember *Three Frogs on a Log*? <u>Nothing happens until action is taken</u>).

Finally, it is the time for you to embark on the journey, using the Roadmap to find Profitable Growth and following the four paths—to The Intersection. It is in your best interest and that of all your stakeholders, your partners, and your people to do this quickly—before competitors do it. But you have an advantage now—you have a roadmap and know where to look—and how to get there. You know how the four paths lead to The Intersection, and how the Roadmap leads to Profitable Growth. Start right away; don't wait; there is a treasure awaiting you. Go after it!

THE END

(OK—that's all. Put the book down and "jump off that log.")

BONUS FEATURE FROM:

RISK MANAGEMENT IN AN UNCERTAIN WORLD: STRATEGIES FOR CRISIS MANAGEMENT.

Published by Bloomsbury Publishing Plc., London, 2012

To purchase the book, contact Macmillan Distribution Limited on 01256 302699 or email: direct@macmillan.co.uk. For full details and to order online, visit www.acblack.com

The Missing Metrics: Managing the Cost and Risk of Complexity

By **John L. Mariotti,** President and CEO of
The Enterprise Group, Powell, OH, USA

Highlights

- Despite the best efforts in many areas, the accounting and finance systems currently in use overlook the costs of complexity—it's all talk and too little action.

- Complexity costs are hidden, buried in the accounts of a company until the period-end statements reflect the adverse effects on profitability.
- The time to recognize that these costs exist, is now, to identify them, and to find or develop new metrics to take the place of those that have been missing for far too long.

Introduction

Accounting systems have come a long way in the past decades. Activity-based costing revealed where costs were being incurred and what was driving them. The blizzard of regulations following debacles involving Enron, WorldCom, etc., led to the passage of the Sarbanes–Oxley Act. The most recent financial crisis spawned The Dodd–Frank Wall Street Reform and Consumer Protection Act, which will undoubtedly lead to many more new regulations (in the United States).

These burdensome new laws impose some necessary disciplines on finance and accounting, but fail to deal with a huge, unmeasured and unmanaged area—the costs of complexity. When I began studying this area in earnest about a decade ago, I discovered just how far reaching the negative impact of complexity has grown, and how much it has gone unnoticed. Certainly there is discussion of complexity, but following all the talk, there is very little organized action.

Back in 2001, Oracle CEO Larry Ellison described a "War on Complexity" in computer software. There were simply too many systems that were not integrated, and others that were very difficult to integrate. This fragmentation of systems caused huge complexity, duplication of effort, and waste (which Ellison's Oracle Corporation hoped to solve).

In 2006-2008 there was another flurry of reports and articles from major consultancies (Bain, McKinsey) and university publications (Wharton, Harvard). More recently, IBM's May 2010 report described a comprehensive survey of 1500 CEOs, which confirmed the breadth, depth, magnitude risks of complexity and how dangerous it is to business around the world. And yet, words have not been converted into action effectively, and complexity management continues to be situational and far from fully effective. A great opportunity still awaits global business.

Variety Can Add Value—If Managed Properly

There are clearly instances when complexity—properly managed—can be a source of great competitive advantage. In these cases, the organization's structure, systems, and processes must be carefully designed to minimize transaction cost and make complexity manageable.

One notable success using complexity for competitive advantage is the web retailer Amazon, whose breadth of offering is extensive, and growing, thus making it a "one-stop shopping" site for millions. Amazon's distribution system, however, is always at risk of being overwhelmed by complexity, even as its front-end systems handle the huge variety of goods seamlessly.

Similarly, US sandwich seller Subway assembles sandwiches to order from 30-40 containers of meat, cheese, and vegetables, using just a dozen varieties of breads and wraps. Thus it can make-to-order millions of sandwiches (and salad), with minimal waste, and great flexibility.

There are many other examples like these two. All depend on the right systemic design to keep complexity from growing out of control, causing harmful, costly waste and inefficiency.

Complexity Costs Are Hidden

When I first researched why complexity costs remained unmeasured in so many companies, I discovered that it was because these costs are, by their nature, hidden by conventional accounting systems. To bring the problem into perspective, consider how complexity occurs and what kinds of waste result. It will become apparent how financial systems simply overlook complexity's costs—until the end-of-period reporting shows the detrimental effects and true costs.

There is no doubt that complexity's effects are readily apparent in monthly, quarterly, and year-end results, where they reduce income and impact the balance sheet adversely. Unfortunately, this is too often the only time and place where they are visible. Even then, there's no indication of how or where these costs were incurred, or how to manage/minimize them.

Seeking High Growth in Low Growth Markets

So much of the complexity that goes unmeasured and unmanaged is created with the best of intentions, in search of revenue growth. Many developed countries (the United States, Europe, Japan, etc.) are growing very slowly, in population and economically. When companies seek growth in such mature markets, they resort to proliferation, which leads to complexity. The gain in revenue is redistributed across a broader range of products and services, with only modest increases in total revenue. The many resulting new products, customers, markets, and suppliers add much more in complexity costs than in profit. As rapidly growing economies like China slow, even slightly, complexity costs will start to impact them as well.

Mergers and acquisitions are another source of complexity. If either of the two combined companies is burdened with complexity (most are), this will transfer to the merger. If both are thus burdened, real trouble is likely. Simply combining the DNA of two companies is a daunting task without struggling under a burden of being "infected" with complexities of two different "strains." There are issues of product and customer overlap, organizational and/or facility redundancy and, inevitable information systems redundancies. When these are combined with cultural conflicts that must be sorted out, the problems become almost insurmountable. This is one of the main reasons why mergers seldom lead to long-term growth in shareholder value.

Less developed countries typically grow at much higher rates (China, India, Brazil, etc.). Emerging consumer societies with favourable balances of trade fuel their economic growth. There's a different complexity problem here: most of these countries save more and spend less—both as consumers and as governments. Further, these countries are less familiar to sellers who operate in developed countries, and therefore marketing and operating mistakes are made. These mistakes also lead to proliferation, often due to errors in targeting, product configuration, branding and/or how to serve the targeted markets and customers.

Profits Are Proportional to Revenues; Costs Are Proportional to Transactions

Thus, either approach to growth adds to complexity, but for different reasons, and in different ways. Profits are derived from increased revenues, but costs are incurred from increased transactions. Therein lies the root of the complexity problems. A few simple reports can expose the problem, but more sophisticated solutions are needed later. Starting with the simpler metrics is advisable. (More on "simplicity" later.)

First, calculate sales per customer, per product, per location, etc., and track the trends. They are typically declining, indicating more transactions for less revenue. Next, sort the annual sales, profits, etc., for customers and products, in descending order of value, and compute a cumulative column. Now look at the bottom of the list. There is always page after page of "losers" with few sales and low or negative profits. These are candidates for a major "housecleaning."

Few accounting systems calculate a couple of simple, yet important, measures. What is the cost to process a customer order from "end to end"—from receipt of the order until the payment is in the bank? Few, if any, companies know the answer to this question. One US study, performed by Sterling Commerce a few years ago, calculated it to be approximately $50. Consider the following quick calculation to show how complexity adds cost and waste.

Many companies make about 5% net profit (after tax) on sales revenue. That means $20 of sales will generate $1 of net profit. If processing an order costs $50, they need a $1,000 order to earn the equivalent of what it costs to process the order. If that type of customer orders every week, $50,000 worth of annual sales barely generates net profit equal to the cost of processing the orders.

This dramatically illustrates how customer orders that are small and frequent can add complexity cost, and yet this cost remains unmeasured and undetected as a drain on profit. A similar comparison could be made for the cost to process purchase orders, or the expense to set up/maintain documentation for a product or service. Nowhere are these costs measured this way and thus they remain unmanaged. Most companies have departments performing these functions. Totalling those departmental expenses and dividing by the total number of orders processed will yield an adequate approximation of the cost to process each order. Yet, few companies do this calculation—or consider its impact.

Complexity costs are also insidious because most of them are hidden in "catch-all" accounts such as variances, allowances and deductions, premium freight, need for overtime labour, scrap and rework, closeout pricing, and so forth. Extra effort is needed to reveal the origin of such entries (more on that later).

Consider a simple example of how easily complexity can occur and grow.

A Simple Example: One White Coffee Mug

Imagine a coffee mug in one style, color, size, and type of packaging; sourced from one supplier, packaged and stocked in one location; and offered for sale to one customer. If the mug's total landed "standard cost" is $1 and it sells for $2, this yields a 50% gross profit margin.

Because the mug is successful, the company expands the line to four styles, four colours, two sizes, and two package options. There are now 64 different variations, which lead to complexity (and errors) in forecasting, buying, controlling, and managing inventory, etc. The "standard cost," however, is still the same as before: cost = $1, price = $2, and gross profit margin = 50%. *But something is wrong.* Intuitively, you know that there are complexity costs that the old metrics don't capture—at least, not included in the "standard cost" and gross profit margin calculation. The true profitability is not nearly the same as before—it is lower, maybe much lower.

Success in revenue growth leads to expansion of the product line again: two suppliers, packaging and inventory in three locations, and sell into three more countries (or markets). Assuming no difference in purchase cost or productivity, the standard cost, price, and gross profit margin remain the same. But now, the number of combinations and permutations has grown to over a thousand. Many different marketing materials are needed; the risk of purchasing/forecast errors grows with demand volatility, and so on. Now the true profitability is clearly lowered again—complexity has struck.

Add colours, mixes and assortments of product that vary by market, customer, production plant, distribution centre, and country, and the warehouses fill with products in the wrong colours or styles, wrong package sizes, etc. Something must be done with these oddments, so they are repacked (cost variance) and sold at discounts (price variance), and replacements are flown in (huge freight expense variances) to meet customer service needs. More profit disappears into those "catch-all" accounts. The accounting standard gross margin has remained essentially unchanged.

Complexity creates increases in overhead and administrative expenses; in the reserves for inventory obsolescence; and/or incurs additional labour to rework, repack, and remark inventory. Few of these costs impact the standard cost and the standard gross margin. Thus, the product still appears to be nicely profitable. The complexity costs remain hidden in undifferentiated accounts—or result in "non-recurring charges," which, mysteriously, seem to "recur" from time to time. At the end of accounting periods, the true costs hit with full impact, in many cases wiping out all profit.

A Complexity Crisis Calls for Metrics

I call this sequence of events "a complexity crisis." The finance and accounting metrics, intended to help track the results of the company do so—eventually. Unfortunately, the waste from complexity remains unmanaged; the missing metrics do not reveal the problems. They are seen only after the fact. Complexity strikes like a robber. A crime has been committed; the money is gone. Clues to the crime are few, and the perpetrators plead innocence and good intentions. Only a knowledgeable accountant, with help from supply chain or marketing staff can unearth the clues and track the loss of money back to its root causes.

The solution for this is evident: to devise and implement the "missing metrics." Many are easy to create; some are already in use. Others will require whole new initiatives (described later). If new metrics were in place and tracked regularly, such losses would be found much sooner. Then corrective actions could be started sooner as well. Major public accounting companies could help by sanctioning such metrics, to provide some uniformity. Unfortunately, thus far, they have been unresponsive to those needs. (Perhaps they are too busy with new governmental regulations and compliance to watch out for the client company's profits.)

Typical Missing Metrics

- Sales per product stock keeping unit (SKU);
- Sales per product category;
- Sales per customer;
- Sales per location;
- Sales per employee (hourly, including full-time equivalent, salaried, and total);
- Sales per part number (components, materials, work in process, and finished goods (FG)).
- Gross profit per product SKU;
- Gross profit per product category;
- Gross profit per customer;
- Gross profit per location.
- Purchases per vendor;
- Purchases per commodity type;
- Production (output value) per person-hour (or equivalent measure of labour input);
- Total number of SKUs by division or business unit and company total;
- Number of SKUs added and dropped during the last time period (quarterly, semi-annually or annually).
- Cost to process a customer order (end to end);
- Cost to process a purchase order (end to end);
- Cost to set up and maintain a product SKU;
- Cost to serve by customer (including freight, handling, and order processing costs).

Within "catchall accounts" like Deductions and Allowances, Variances, and write-offs for Obsolescence, add subcategories to segregate entries by major customers (or groups), products (or categories), and locations (divisions).

- Expenses per product line or category;
- Expenses per customer, and/or by customer type/category;
- Expenses per location;
- Percentage of sales per product line or category;
- Percentage of sales per customer, and customer type or category.

Plus Totally New Metric—The Complexity Factor (CF) and New Tools

Obviously, there is a common overall purpose among these metrics. Remember that the objective of new metrics is to reveal where the costs of complexity are hiding and are wasting time and money. Choose among those that measure similar complexity-related outcomes. Finally, an overall Complexity Factor can be calculated by the following formula (where "locations" are meaningful facilities and "countries" are places where legal entities exist):

(No. of suppliers + No. of customers + No. of employees) × No. of FG SKUs × No. of markets served × No. of locations × No. of countries ÷ Total annual sales revenue (in the company currency of choice)

The resultant number provides a "benchmark," called a Complexity Factor (CF), for the business (or subunit) whose data were used to calculate it. Obviously, a CF can be calculated for each business unit, division, geographical unit, etc. *and* for the entire company.

This may seem like a large number of new metrics, but the data to compile them should already exist. All parts of a company may not need all of the metrics. Different parts of the business should use metrics (including the CF) that are relevant to their activities.

Some much simpler solutions have been developed in two different continents: www.simpler.com in the UK, and www.simplerbusiness.com in Australia. Each offers a range of solutions that focus on simplicity instead of complexity. Whichever direction you choose to manage complexity will use largely similar approaches and metrics—find where the complexity resides, how much it costs, and then drive it out and manage it. Complexity is like weeds in a garden. Removing it once is insufficient. It comes back. It must be constantly measured and managed.

When more sophisticated, analytical solutions are needed, new ones have been developed by Emcien (www.emcien.com), which analyses and optimizes complex patterns/assortments, and by Ontonix (www.ontonix.com), which also measures risk. As complexity grows, an organization can be overwhelmed by it, and lose control of the company. This is a catastrophic failure and must be avoided at all costs. The OntoNet™ system analyses complexity in terms of risk and the fragility of an entity, and can be applied for a wide range of situations. This kind of solution is the ultimate "insurance policy missing metric"—complexity risk.

What Gets Measured, Gets Managed; What Doesn't, Doesn't

The mere presence of metrics doesn't mean management will do anything differently. On the other hand, the absence of metrics virtually assures that nothing will be done. The old line "What gets measured, gets managed," is true. The opposite, "If you can't—or don't—measure it, you can't—or don't—manage it," is also likely to be true. Talk and studies do not solve problems; only action does.

Measurement alone also doesn't solve any problems either. It merely points to the nature of those problems. To manage complexity requires a series of steps from simpler to more sophisticated.

First, use Pareto's Principle (the 80-20 rule). Sort products and customers in descending order of annual revenues and profits, and carefully analyze the bottom of the list. Most are "losers" with a few strategically important "potential winners" scattered about. Getting rid of the losers is imperative.

Upgrading a few "losers" into "winners" (top 20%) is possible, but for most, it is impractical. In the middle group careful analysis helps choose potential winners for upgrading and imminent losers downgrading and removal.

When more powerful tools are needed, the newly devised, more powerful tools and systems (Emcien, Ontonix) can help greatly in sorting, selection, and optimization of complex situations.

The Time for New Metrics Is Now

Now is the time for boards of directors, senior management, and accounting and finance organizations around the globe to recognize the huge cost of complexity and how poorly measured and managed it is. The waste of time and money due to "missing metrics" and the failure to track and manage complexity are immense, costing companies around the globe billions in profits. Now is the time to stop that waste in its tracks—by installing those "missing metrics" —and then acting on the new information and knowledge they provide

More Info
Books:
George, Michael L., and Stephen A. Wilson. *Conquering Complexity in Your Business*. New York: McGraw-Hill, 2004.

Mariotti, John. *The Complexity Crisis: Why Too Many Products, Markets, and Customers Are Crippling Your Company—And What to Do About It.* Avon, MA: Adams Media, 2008.

Articles:
Berlind, David. "Oracle: Misquoted, misunderstood." *ZDnet Tech Update* (September 6, 2001). Online at: <u>tinyurl.com/3usfr6a</u>

Gottfredson, Mark, and Keith Aspinall. "Innovation versus complexity: What is too much of a good thing?" *Harvard*

Business Review 83:11 (November 2005): 62–71. Online at: tinyurl.com/3lkanaw

Heywood, Suzanne, Jessica Spungin, and David Turnbull. "Cracking the complexity code." *McKinsey Quarterly* (May 2007): 85–95.

Reports:

A.T. Kearney. "Waging war on complexity: How to master the matrix organizational structure." 2003.

George Group and Knowledge@Wharton. "Unravelling complexity in products and services." Special report, 2006. Online at: tinyurl.com/3u4lrke

IBM Global Business Services. "Capitalizing on Complexity: Insights from the Chief Executive Officer Study". IBM Global Business Services, Route 100, Somer, NY 10589. USA. May 2010

Resources:

Emcien, optimization tools for complex solutions: www.emcien.com

Ontonix, Complexity and Risk Management tools, www.ontonix.com

Simpler Business resources: www.simplerbusiness.com (Ian Dover, Principal, Australia) and www.simpler.com (Mark Hafer, CEO, UK)

About the Author

John L. Mariotti is founder, President & CEO of **The Enterprise Group** a coalition of *time-shared advisors*™ which he founded 18 years go, after having been formerly President of Huffy Bicycles and of Rubbermaid Office Products Group. He is also previously Chairman of World Kitchen, LLC, on whose board he still serves.

John has written eight business books, a mini-book, and a novel, as well as hundreds of articles and columns. Two of his books, *The Shape Shifters—Continuous Change for Com-*

petitive Advantage (Wiley 1997) and *The Complexity Crisis* (Adams Media 2008) were award winners. *The Shape Shifters* was named one of 1997's Most Innovative books for leaders, and *The Complexity Crisis* was chosen as one of 2008's Best Business Books, and one of 2008's Best Books for Small Business. His latest book, *Hope is NOT a Strategy: Leadership Lessons from the Obama Presidency* was co-authored with D. M. Lukas.

Mariotti serves on corporate boards, advises/consults with companies and does public speaking. In the past, he was a regular columnist for IndustryWeek, Fortune Small Business (www.fsb.com), and The American Management Association (www.AMAnet.org) and has written for www.Forbes.com, and American Express' www.openforum.com, along with many other print publications, as well as for numerous web sites and blogs.

Since 2001, John has published a private weekly e-newsletter: THE ENTERPRISE, which is posted on his blog: http://mariotti.blogs.com/my_weblog/. He continues to contribute to other blogs as well, including most recently, www.thebrennerbrief.com. John lives in Ohio, and can be reached at www.mariotti.net/

Acknowledgements:

A special thanks to Mike Harris and Jim Marra whose editing of the manuscript added immeasurably to its content and readability. Also thanks are due to Phil Rist and Gary Drenik, who reminded me about the importance of information, which caused that section to be added and improved significantly. Thanks to Chrissy Wissinger and Stephanie Blakely of BIGinsight for their help.

I would also like to thank Joe Seladi, then CEO of Amrep, who let me use this material with his company's strategic planning process—while it was still "in development." Last, I would like to thank my many friends and colleagues who, over the years, have contributed ideas and thoughts on the topic while it was under development.

(I'd try to list them all, but I am afraid I would leave someone out.)

Thanks to you all.

Made in the USA
Lexington, KY
16 April 2016